15185

W9-BZS-623

MAHS

REFERENCE

CULTURES OF THE WORLD

HUNGARY

Richard S. Esbenshade

MARSHALL CAVENDISH
New York • London • Sydney

Reference edition published 1994 by
Marshall Cavendish Corporation
2415 Jerusalem Avenue
P.O. Box 587
North Bellmore
New York 11710

© Times Editions Pte Ltd 1994

Originated and designed by
Times Books International, an imprint of
Times Editions Pte Ltd

Printed in Malaysia

Library of Congress Cataloging-in-Publication Data:
Esbenshade, Richard S.
    Hungary / Richard S. Esbenshade. — Reference ed.
        p. cm.—(Cultures Of The World)
    Includes bibliographical references and index.
    ISBN 1-85435-588-0
        1. Hungary—Juvenile literature. [1. Hungary.] I. Title.
II. Series.
DB906.E83 1994
943.9—dc20   93–45746
                        CIP
                            AC

Cultures of the World

Editorial Director	Shirley Hew
Managing Editor	Shova Loh
Editors	Tan Kok Eng
	Roseline Lum
	Michael Spilling
	Winnifred Wong
	Guek-Cheng Pang
	Sue Sismondo
Picture Editor	Mee-Yee Lee
Production	Edmund Lam
Design	Tuck Loong
	Ronn Yeo
	Felicia Wong
	Loo Chuan Ming
Illustrators	Eric Chew
	Lok Kerk Hwang
	William Sim
	Wong Nok Sze
MCC Editorial Director	Evelyn M. Fazio

INTRODUCTION

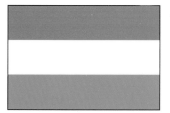

An extremely proud people, Hungarians value their unique language and distinctive customs. Their literary and artistic traditions show a passionate commitment to their culture, as well as a knack for knowing when to adapt, when to secretly subvert, and when to openly rebel. Often reserved and untrusting of outsiders, the Hungarian people are devoted to family and friends and protect a private life that is deep and rich.

Hungary's culture and history put it in a unique position to form a bridge between West and East. Hungarians now hope that the end of Communism and of centuries of domination and social inequality will finally free them to find democracy, independence, and economic well-being. This volume in the *Cultures of the World* series will explore a resourceful people and their response to a history of adversity.

CONTENTS

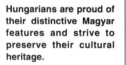

Hungarians are proud of their distinctive Magyar features and strive to preserve their cultural heritage.

CONTENTS

The real charm of Hungary reveals itself in the quiet little cobbled streets where merchants display their wares for sale on the sidewalks.

GEOGRAPHY

SITUATED IN THE LOW-LYING CARPATHIAN BASIN between the Alps and the Carpathian Mountains, Hungary has been continually overrun by conquering armies from East and West. In times of peace, traders and travelers have brought new political ideas and fostered cultural innovation.

Until the end of World War I, the kingdom of Hungary extended from the snowy peaks of the Carpathian Mountains to the shore of the Adriatic Sea. However, the 1920 Treaty of Trianon that concluded the war stripped Hungary of over 70% of its territory, leaving a small, flat, landlocked country. Although this loss caused the Hungarian people much soul-searching, present-day Hungary—characterized by plains, fields, rivers, and lakes—retains its distinctive charms.

Opposite: **At the Danube Bend, north of Budapest, the river makes a wide curve south. Some of Hungary's most beautiful scenery can be seen here.**

Below: **Transdanubia, between the Danube and the Austrian border, is still an agricultural region despite the presence of many mining operations.**

A FLAT COUNTRY

One advantage of having a flat land surface is that Hungary is almost self-sufficient in food production and even exports such commodities as corn and beets.

Although Hungary is usually described as an "Eastern European" country, it is actually located near the geographical center of Europe. Hungarians like to think of themselves as "Central European," an integral part of the continent and its culture. The country is 35,907 square miles in area, roughly the size of Indiana. It is about 325 miles from west to east and 155 miles from north to south. The Danube River in the northwest, the Ipel in the north, and the Mur and Drava rivers in the southwest make up part of Hungary's borders. Hungary's neighbors are Austria to the west, Slovakia to the north, Ukraine (formerly U.S.S.R.) and Romania to the east, and Serbia, Croatia, and Slovenia (all formerly Yugoslavia) to the south and southwest. The great political changes taking place in the region since 1989 have altered the names and identities of Hungary's neighbors, but have left its borders intact.

Hungary lies in a geographic formation called the "middle Danube depression." Dominated by the largest plain in Europe, about two-thirds of the area is almost completely flat and less than 650 feet in elevation. Hungary retains some small mountain ranges, but its highest peak, Mt. Kékes, measures only 3,330 feet. Nevertheless, Hungarians have turned this dull configuration to their advantage by putting more than half of their land area under cultivation—more than twice the European average.

What lies below ground is also noteworthy. In Hungary the temperature

below ground increases by one degree every 36.5 feet in depth compared to the norm elsewhere, of one degree every 54.5 to 60 feet. This thermal activity explains the presence of the numerous mineral springs that have been used for bathing and therapy for centuries. The earth also yields substantial mineral resources: coal, magnesium, uranium, copper, lead, zinc, and large amounts of bauxite, which is used in making aluminum.

CLIMATE

Hungary lies at the intersection of three major climatic zones: the Atlantic coast climate is mild and oceanic; the Mediterranean climate brings rainy winters and hot, dry summers; and the extreme Asiatic climate blows dry winds in from the Russian steppes. This means that Hungary's climate may change from year to year, as one or the other of these types predominates. Temperatures range from 25°F to 72°F, with the annual mean at 50°F. Average rainfall per year is 25 inches, generally higher in the western part of the country, but that is also unpredictable.

THE MUTILATED MOTHERLAND

All Hungarians, no matter what their social class or political stance, were deeply shocked and hurt by the loss of over two-thirds of their country's territory in the Paris peace settlement following World War I. Some 3.5 million of their fellow Magyars—one-third of the total population—found themselves residents of neighboring countries. In succeeding decades, the slogan "Small Hungary, no country; Big Hungary, heaven!" became a nationalist rallying cry. Although Hitler rewarded Hungary for allying with Germany by restoring much of the lost territories in 1938 and 1940, these were taken away again at the end of World War II, as Hungary once more was on the losing side.

Even today, Hungarians retain a strong feeling for these areas and the ethnic Hungarians who continue to live there—some 600,000 in Slovakia, 200,000 in Ukraine, 1.7 to 2.5 million (depending on who is counting) in Transylvania (Romania), and 500,000 in Serbia. They still use the old Hungarian names for the territories and their towns—Felvidék ("FEL-vee-dayk") or "upper country" for Slovakia, Erdély ("AIR-day") for Transylvania, Délvidék ("DAYL-vee-dayk") or "southern country" for Serbia, and Vajdaság ("VAI-dah-shaahg") for Voivodina in Serbia. Despite these emotional ties, most Hungarians recognize political realities and do not support border changes. The neighboring countries, however, are quick to accuse Hungarians of wanting their old lands back; a statement by former Prime Minister József Antall that he considered himself "Prime Minister of all the Hungarians" only increased this concern.

THE HUNGARIAN PLAIN

To the east of the Danube river stretches the *puszta* ("POO-stah"), a vast, apparently empty flatland that forms the heart of Hungary, both physically and spiritually. Like the expanses of the American Midwest, beneath the seeming emptiness lie both wealth and character. When the original Magyar tribes swept into the Hungarian Basin in the ninth century, they found this area of wild grasslands ideal for shepherding and horse breeding, their traditional activities. After the semi-nomadic peoples decided to settle down, they planted vineyards and fruit trees, and so began the gradual transformation of barren land into a Central European breadbasket. The driving of huge cattle herds to far-off towns in Italy, Germany, and Austria was gradually replaced by a feudal system of agricultural estates, and the *csikós* ("CHEE-kohsh"), the Hungarian cowboy, was replaced by landowning nobles and their peasant serfs.

Today the great majority of the *puszta* is under cultivation, livestock is fenced in, and the only remnants of the *csikós* are those who perform for foreign tourists. But parts of the *puszta*, especially around Hortobágy, retain an elusive, almost mystical charm: subtle coloration, delicate natural balance, sudden and violent changes in weather, the *délibab*("DAY-lee-bahb") or Hungarian mirage, and man-made landmarks such as the *gémeskút* ("GAY-mesh-koot") or *shadoof,* a kind of water-drawing apparatus in the shape of a cross, which can be seen for miles.

The landscape of the *puszta* is punctuated by flocks of white sheep tended by shepherds who still wear traditional costume.

RIVERS AND LAKES

Hungary is defined geographically by rivers and lakes. The river systems of the Danube (Duna, "DOO-nah," in Hungarian) and the Tisza ("TEE-sah") spread out over much of Hungary's territory. Irrigation provided by these two rivers has turned barren grasslands into fertile farmland. The western geographical region, between the Danube and the Austrian border (the other two main regions are the Great Plain and the Northern Uplands), is called Transdanubia—"across the Danube." The area east of the Tisza has traditionally been referred to as Tiszántúl ("TEE-sahn-tool"), "on the far side of the Tisza." In the past, seasonal flooding by the rivers and their tributaries put much of the surrounding countryside at constant risk of destruction. Flood control measures have now been put in place and there is little risk of flooding.

Hungary's lakes are dominated by Lake Balaton, the largest lake in Central Europe; the other main lakes are Lake Velence and Lake Fertö (most of which extends into Austria, where it is called Neusiedler See). Located about halfway between the Danube and the country's western border, and about one hour from the capital, Lake Balaton is easily accessible to tourists from Western Europe; over one-third of Hungary's tourist revenue comes from Balaton. Covering an area of 160 square miles, Lake Balaton is very shallow, averaging only 10 feet deep, with a maximum depth of 35 feet; the surface freezes completely in the winter. The lake has been called a "surrogate sea" for landlocked Hungary, as it moderates temperatures and affects rainfall. In addition to recreational resorts, Balaton's environs harbor unique wetlands, some of which are protected nature reserves for birds. But industrial development, growth of algae, sewage disposal, acid rain, and the draining of the Little Balaton marsh have endangered the Balaton environment.

THE BLUE DANUBE

Most Westerners think of Austria when they hear about the romantic Danube, but it is in Hungary that the river is perhaps most beautiful. The Danube and its eight bridges form the very heart of Budapest, cutting the city in two and providing a majestic panorama, which has been declared an international cultural treasure by UNESCO. In the Danube Bend area north of Budapest, where the river takes its great turn to the south, spectacular fortifications, islands, and historic towns can be seen on both banks. The river also provides a major navigational route suitable for ocean-going vessels from Budapest south to Belgrade, in Serbia, and then east through Romania and Bulgaria to its mouth in the Black Sea.

From Budapest to the Serbian border, the river drops less than six inches per mile, resulting in a slow-moving, gradual course. But this moderation is deceptive: the Danube has often spawned destructive flooding. "Ice plugs" can develop when the ice begins to break up, but is

restrained by the still-frozen river downstream. The river then bursts through the "plugs" in a powerful barrage of water and ice; such an occurrence wiped out most of the capital (then still three separate cities) in 1838. In 1879, the seasonal second or "green" flood period ("green" because the ice has melted, in contrast to the earlier wintry "white" flood) swelled the Danube to the point where it could not absorb the Tisza's waters, causing a backup on the Tisza that flooded and destroyed the historic city of Szeged. Flooding is rarer now, but the other extreme, drought, can cause dangerously low water levels: in the summer of 1992, heat and dry conditions caused normal river traffic to be stopped for several weeks, and Budapest's water supply was threatened.

FLORA AND FAUNA

Centuries of cultivation of the land and transformation of nature have all but eliminated Hungary's original environment. Most of the forests have disappeared, and only 10–15% of the land area is still characterized by natural vegetation; the locust is the only remaining species of large tree. Wildlife, such as the wild boar of Hungarian folktales, has dwindled as its environment has shrunk. However, the boar and some species of deer are now protected as game animals. A few wolves and lynx may still survive in the mountainous areas, but the wild horses of the *puszta* are now gone. Black buffaloes, bred for milk, were once seen in the area southwest of Balaton; now only a small herd remains, on a reserve visited by tourists.

Bird populations are much more successful, especially in and around Balaton, and other lakes and wetlands; the species one may encounter include egrets, herons, storks, spoonbills, cormorants, ospreys, and bustards, as well as hawks and the occasional eagle. The numerous fish in the lakes and streams include European carp, perch, pike, and sheatfish (a large freshwater catfish living in Eastern and Central European waters).

At birth, the wild boar is brown with light stripes. But as it grows older, the whole coat becomes a uniform dark brown or black.

CAPITAL, TOWNS, AND VILLAGES

The Hungarian social landscape is dominated by Budapest. Originally three cities—Óbuda, Buda, and Pest—the capital was unified in 1872. It is home to two million residents, one-fifth of Hungary's population, and another million enter the city every day to work or shop. This huge metropolis is a legacy of its days as center of half the Habsburg Empire.

Hungary's second largest city, Debrecen, hardly compares to the sprawling capital. There are seven other cities with populations above 100,000, but most of Hungary's people live in smaller towns, villages, and industrial centers, and they are spread evenly throughout the countryside. Early visitors to Hungary described a vast, Asiatic swampland with huge villages. With the development of agriculture, the system of the *tanya* ("TAHN-yah")—a kind of plantation-estate, very isolated and home to the wretchedly poor farmhands who worked there—predominated. What remains to this day is the sharp contrast between urban and rural living, characterized by romanticization of the countryside by city dwellers on the one hand, and suspicion of the city by peasants on the other.

Budapest is the economic, political, and cultural center of Hungary. At night, the illuminated Chain Bridge casts a romantic glow on the Danube River.

HISTORY

HUNGARIANS SEE THEIR HISTORY as an unending series of tragedies. The country has for centuries been subject to domination, occupation, and devastation by neighboring powers. Still, they are proud of their 1,000-year-old nation, once one of the most advanced in Europe.

THE GREAT MIGRATION

In A.D. 896, the original seven Magyar (ethnic Hungarian) tribes, led by Árpád, crossed the rugged Carpathian mountain passes and entered the Danube Basin, ending a 5,000-year migration from distant Asian steppes. The Magyars found a land populated by a mixture of Slavic, Turkish, and Germanic tribes, whom they quickly conquered and enslaved. Before the fourth century the area had been settled by the Romans.

The Magyars used special stirrups that allowed them to stand and shoot their arrows in any direction while riding full speed. They continued their expeditions far and wide to gather booty and slaves. Said to drink horse blood, the Magyars were feared throughout Europe. In 955, after a crushing defeat at the hands of German Emperor Otto I, they decided not to venture outside the Danube Basin area.

Opposite: **Hungarians worship King Stephen as their first Christian saint. These two statues in Veszprém show the saint king with his wife Queen Gizella.**

Below: **The arrival of the Magyars is depicted in vivid colors by painter Mihály Munkácsy. This painting hangs on the wall of the Munkácsy room in the Hungarian Parliament.**

ST. STEPHEN'S CROWN

The Holy Crown of Hungary, with its double bands and bent cross (see page 73), has become a symbol of Hungarian nationalism. The upper section was sent by Pope Sylvester to Stephen I for his coronation in A.D. 1000, but the lower section, a gift from the emperor of Byzantium, was added by Géza I in 1074. As the Hungarian kingdom expanded, it became the object of struggles for possession by royalty across Europe.

After the Turks took over Byzantium (renamed Constantinople) and launched their offensives against Christian Europe, the crown came to represent the defense of the West and the sacrifice of Hungary in defending the West. Kept in the United States during the early years of Communist rule, the crown and its accessories were returned to Budapest to great fanfare in 1974. In recent years the royal regalia have become a potent symbol of nationalism on the rise.

THE FIRST HUNGARIAN STATE

After their defeat, the Magyars looked around for a favorable alliance. There was a growing rivalry between the Eastern Orthodox Church, based in Byzantium, and the Western Catholic Church, based in Rome. Hungary's leader chose Rome. With the crowning of his son Vajk as King István (Stephen) by the Pope on Christmas Day of the year 1000, Hungary placed itself firmly in the camp of Western culture.

Stephen, the "first European among Hungarians," immediately set about converting his subjects, by force if necessary. His strong hand created a uniform state with an advanced legal code, and the many foreigners he brought into the country created the basis for a multi-ethnic society. He was made a saint after his death, and despite a messy succession struggle, the Hungarian kingdom was solidly grounded for the next five centuries.

THE GOLDEN AGE

Despite bloody struggles for the crown, the country continued to be built up. It benefited from its location astride East-West trade, which encouraged the immigration of skilled and enterprising foreign settlers, strengthening the multi-ethnic nature of the population.

Hungary's progress was abruptly halted by the devastating invasion of the Mongols, led by Batu Khan, in 1241. King Béla IV fled to the coast, and more than half of the population was exterminated. But the invaders retreated as suddenly as they had come, and the country was slowly reconstructed, eventually surpassing its former prosperity.

In 1301, when the Árpád dynasty died out, Charles Robert of the Italian House of Anjou became king of Hungary. He reasserted his kingly power over the landowning magnates, increased trade, and developed agriculture and mining, especially of gold—Hungary at that time produced one-third of the world's gold, and Hungarian gold forints spread throughout Europe. His successor Louis the Great expanded the territory and built a system of grand castles. By the end of the 14th century, Hungary contained 49 cities, over 500 towns, and 21,000 villages, with a population of some three million, despite the ravages of the Black Death (bubonic plague epidemic).

Matthias Corvinus, the last king to reign over the whole of Hungary, brought the full flower of the Italian Renaissance to the country. He set great numbers of book-copiers to work, and built up a library, called Corvina, to rival the greatest of Europe. Unfortunately the Corvina was later destroyed. Matthias brought about economic prosperity, but also raised taxes to foster artistic luxury in his court and to form Hungary's first permanent professional military, called the Black Army. His 1486 Code of Laws put Hungary at the forefront of European legal progress, and earned him the epithet "Matthias the Just."

"The Mongol invasion is said to have been preceded by a number of menacing omens, including ravaging wolfpacks, unusual numbers of deformed newborns, and, finally, a solar eclipse. The invasion itself left 'nothing to be found back in our land, except the bones and skulls of those murdered and destroyed walls of our cities, still red from the blood so freely shed.' "

—Ivan Völgyes, political scientist

Arabic writing above a baptismal font shows the strong Turkish influence in a church in Pécs.

TURKISH AND HABSBURG OCCUPATION

After Matthias's death, Hungary fell to the Turks and the Austrian Habsburg Empire. In 1526, the country was partitioned: central Hungary, including the Great Plain and part of Transdanubia, fell under Turkish rule; the rest of Transdanubia was taken over by the Habsburgs; Transylvania constituted itself as a semi-independent principality under Turkish suzerainty; and the northern Carpathian area fell into a state of anarchy and civil war.

The Turks savagely exploited the land and enslaved the people. The Habsburgs were hardly less cruel: discriminatory tariffs and the preservation of a feudal landholding system kept their part of Hungary poor and backward, and maintained it as a source of cheap raw materials for their growing empire. In addition, constant war between the two powers on Hungarian soil left the country even more devastated.

Transylvania became the symbol of the survival of Hungarian spirit and the preservation of its culture. As the Transylvanian princes were Protestant, Hungarian patriotism came to be identified with Protestantism.

The 17th century was filled with Hungarian independence struggles. The most successful was by the *kuruc* ("KOO-roots," or cross). The *kuruc* army, which took on the character of a peasant rebellion as well as national liberation, succeeded in occupying Upper Hungary and reaching into Austria. Subsequently, under the hero Francis Rákóczy II, it reached the gates of Vienna before being forced to surrender in 1711.

After the failure of the Rákóczy Rebellion, Hungary became tired of fighting and reconciled itself to Habsburg rule. Empress Maria Theresa brought development to the devastated country, building roads and schools, and draining the marshlands; but she would not develop industry, introduce land reform, or allow the reunification of Transylvania with Hungary proper. Moreover, she favored Latin over Hungarian as the language of government.

The situation of the peasantry, oppressed by both imperial rule and Hungarian landlords, became even worse with the growing demand for grain in Western Europe. When Maria Theresa's successor, Joseph II, tried to initiate rational economic and governmental reforms in the guise of an "enlightened absolutism," the Hungarian nobles resisted, citing their historic rights, but in reality fearing the loss of immediate privileges. Joseph relented, and instead of modernization, sought the greatest economic benefit for the empire from taxing the feudal estate system.

JÁNOS HUNYADI AND THE *DÉLI HARANGSZÓ*

János Hunyadi, a 15th-century Hungarian noble and soldier, gained fame throughout Europe as the "scourge of the Turks" for his success in battle against the Ottoman Empire. His finest hour came when he led his forces to meet a massive Turkish army at Nándorfehérvár (now Belgrade in Serbia). Pope Calixtus III, calling Hungary the "shield of Christianity," issued a Papal Bull (an order given by the Pope) decreeing that the bells of every Catholic church be rung daily at noon for a Christian victory. The battle ended in a crushing defeat for the Turks. The noon bell-ringing at churches, which Hungarians call *déli harangszó* ("DAY-lee HAH-rahng-soh"), continues to this day all across the Christian world, in honor of János Hunyadi's victory.

"The Hungarian nobles, who keep you in servitude, do not consider you as citizens, but treat you as slaves. ... Whatever grows on the fields, thanks to your toil and sweat, belongs to them. ... What is left for you is serfdom and misery. ... There is no other way but to exterminate the nobility—or give satisfaction by offering your blood and eternal servitude to our most insolent enemies ..."

—*György Dózsa, leader of the 1514 Rebellion*

THE DÓZSA REBELLION

In 1514, following a papal call to organize a crusade against the Turks, an army was recruited from among Hungary's peasants. The latter joined up in great numbers, in part because of religious fervor, but even more to escape their cruel lot on the landlords' estates. The landlords, needing their labor—the call occurred just at harvest time—and fearing that the army would turn against them, began using force to prevent their serfs from joining. This in turn aroused the peasants even more against their masters. Led by a Transylvanian lower nobleman named György Dózsa, they declared a "crusade" against the "wicked nobility" and began destroying the large estates.

The nobles raised an army of their own and, after four months, defeated Dózsa's large but ragged forces. Dózsa, the "peasant king," was forced to sit on a white-hot iron throne, with a glowing crown and scepter, and his followers were forced to eat his charred flesh before being killed in turn—a kind of violent retribution characteristic of Hungarian history. The nobles' revenge against the peasants took some 70,000 lives. As if this were not enough, the nobles passed legislation equating the Hungarian nation with only the free noble class, tying the peasantry to the land and depriving them of rights for all time. The sharp alienation of the peasantry from the upper classes remains, to some degree, to this day. György Dózsa was glorified by the post-World War II Communist rulers, with statues in his honor and streets named after him in towns across Hungary.

GROWTH OF NATIONAL CONSCIOUSNESS

In the 19th century nationalism spread across Europe. In Hungary, the national renaissance began with an exploration of the native Magyar contributions to Hungarian history. An intellectual stratum grew out of the lower and middle nobility, favoring the use of Hungarian over Latin and German. They were concerned over the social and economic development of the nation. By the time of the "First Reform Generation" of the 1830s, the rich landowners had begun to realize that Hungary's increasing backwardness and poverty were harming them too, and that reform was necessary for modernization.

The two most prominent Hungarian statesmen of the 19th century, Count István Széchenyi and Lajos Kossuth, both now celebrated as national heroes, are a study in contrasts. Széchenyi was a practical, realistic liberal reformer who dedicated himself to building up the country and its inner strength; he believed steady pressure on the government by an educated people was the most effective way to achieve reform. Kossuth was a national revolutionary with a romantic vision; he wanted to unleash the masses against the enemies of the nation. Széchenyi had grave misgivings about Kossuth's radical course, but it was Kossuth's Freedom Struggle of 1848 that eventually led to a short-lived Hungarian liberation.

At the Battle of Timisoara, the 1848 revolutionaries suffered a great defeat that made it impossible for them to continue their insurrection against the Austrian occupiers. (Timisoara is now a part of Romania.)

REVOLUTION AND COMPROMISE

On March 15, 1848, the poet Sándor Petőfi recited a poem called *National Song* to a group of young men in a Pest-Buda (the capital's old name) café, setting off the Hungarian national revolution. The same day, Kossuth arrived in Vienna to meet with the emperor; he was granted his radical reforms, and a virtually independent Hungarian government was installed.

However, by the end of the year, the revolutionary tide had ebbed, and the Austrian rulers were ready to take their revenge. The powerful imperial army descended on Pest-Buda and smothered the new state. Kossuth and his followers retreated to eastern Hungary, and in a stunning turnaround, the Hungarian army drove out the Austrians from their capital. But at this point geopolitics intervened: the young Habsburg emperor Franz Joseph urgently requested assistance from Tsar Nicholas of Russia, and the huge Russian army marched in to put an end to the independence revolution. Hungary was subjected to a merciless and humiliating occupation. Kossuth spent the rest of his long life in exile, agitating for Hungarian independence. Count Széchenyi, on the other hand, ended up in an insane asylum in Austria, where he committed suicide some years later.

By the 1860s, Austria's hold on Hungary had been weakened by passive resistance on the part of the Hungarians, tensions among other nationalities within the empire, and a weakening international position. The Hungarian statesman Ferenc Deák, a brilliant constitutionalist and indefatigable negotiator, pressed Emperor Franz Joseph for concessions. After the Prussian army defeated the Austrians in 1866, the emperor realized that, more than anything, he needed stability and peace at home, and the next year he agreed to the *Ausgleich*, or balancing, in which Hungary became an equal partner in the empire, with effective sovereignty over the large territory allotted to it.

The "K.u.K. period" (*Kaiser und König*, German for Emperor and King) lasted until the outbreak of World War I in 1914. Hungarian culture flourished, and a relatively liberal and democratic political order was established. Jews and other minorities were invited to adopt the Magyar language and culture, and thus be considered fully Hungarian and equal citizens. This "generous" gesture was in effect forcible assimilation, and the minorities as a whole were excluded from political power. In addition, the nobles retained their privileged position, and the peasant masses remained in squalor and misery. But this was ignored in the whirl of progress: in 1896, the 1,000-year anniversary of the Magyar tribes' migration was celebrated with an exposition and the inauguration of the first subway line on the European continent, and the "Second Reform Generation" developed plans to modernize the economic and political system.

THE POET-LIBERATOR

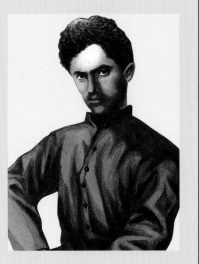

Sándor Petőfi was barely 25 years old when he inspired the peaceful March 15 uprising in Budapest. Petőfi joined the national army and was killed in battle against the invading Russians on July 31, 1849. He had a premonition of his fate, expressed in his poem *One Thought Torments Me*, which includes the lines: "Let me die on that battlefield. Let my young blood flow there from my heart. ... And above my corpse wheezing horses will trot off to the well-deserved victory, leaving me trampled to death." His poetry was lyrical and mixed romantic love with freedom and nationalistic feelings. Every young Hungarian knows his poem *Freedom, Love* by heart. Petőfi remains a national hero and martyr.

WORLD WAR I

The outbreak of World War I put an abrupt end to K.u.K. prosperity. Hungary entered the war on the side of the Central Powers and suffered a crushing defeat at the hands of the Allies.

In the chaos of wartime, movements for radical social and political change arose. At the end of the war, a bourgeois democratic revolution swept Count Mihály Károlyi into power in Budapest. However, he resigned soon after, and a Bolshevik regime headed by Béla Kun took over. Four months later, the landowner class, who had formed an army under Admiral Miklós Horthy, combined forces with the Romanian army to drive Kun and his fanatical followers out.

Exhausted and dejected, Hungarian troops return to Budapest from the front lines in 1918.

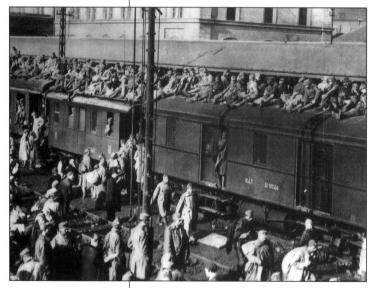

Subsequently, the Treaty of Trianon deprived Hungary of more than two-thirds of its territory and about 3.5 million ethnic Hungarians. American President Woodrow Wilson's declaration of the self-determination of nations guaranteed the right of Czechs, Slovaks, Romanians, Serbs, and Croats to be joined with their new countries, but Hungarians felt that they were not being given the same right, since large numbers of Magyars along Hungary's borders were left in neighboring countries (Czechoslovakia, Romania, and Yugoslavia) for political or strategic reasons. This injustice tortured the Hungarian soul for the next two decades.

INTERWAR HUNGARY AND WORLD WAR II

In the early 1930s, young writers and students from the populist movement went to the countryside to investigate the wretched lifestyle of the peasants. They celebrated the peasants as the suffering "true Magyars" and called for radical land reform and social justice. In the capital, cosmopolitan writers agitated for a free press, a democratic government, and workers' rights. At the same time, growing anti-Semitic feelings (hatred of Jews) fed the fascist Arrow Cross movement. The Horthy regime resisted the pressures from both left and right, falling however more and more under the sway of Germany, from which Hungary hoped for aid in regaining its lost territories.

Germany annexed Austria in 1934, and in October 1938, Nazi leader Adolf Hitler got the other European powers to agree to his plan to break up Czecho-slovakia. Hungary was rewarded for its support with the gift of most of the area it had lost to Czechoslovakia 18 years earlier. Hitler gave Transylvania back in 1940, and the territories in Yugoslavia in 1941. In return, Hungary had to send troops to fight with the Germans. Meanwhile, Hungary's leaders, realizing that Germany was losing the war, opened secret negotiations with the Allies. Hitler found out, and the German army occupied Hungary in March 1944 and installed their Arrow Cross friends in power. The Soviets invaded later that year and, after a destructive battle for Budapest, "liberated" the country on April 4, 1945.

These Hungarian troops near Budapest could do nothing to spare their capital: the city was badly damaged by both the German and the Soviet army.

HUNGARIAN JEWS DURING WORLD WAR II

In 1938, under German pressure, Hungary passed the first of its anti-Jewish laws, which prohibited marriage with non-Jews, limited the number of Jews admitted to the universities, and put other restrictions on Jewish participation in social and economic life. But, through the first years of the war, as the Nazis were exterminating Europe's Jews, the Jewish people in Hungary were for the most part not physically harmed.

After the Germans invaded Hungary, they ordered the deportation of the "Jewish vermin." Within a few months, Hungarian police led by fanatical Arrow Cross militants packed hundreds of thousands of Jews—and Gypsies too—into freight cars and sent them to their deaths at Auschwitz and other Nazi camps. The Jews of Budapest, who had played a prominent role in the city's social, economic, and cultural life, were to be deported last. But by then the Soviet army was already nearing the capital. The heroic efforts of Raoul Wallenberg, a Swedish diplomat, saved thousands of Jews: he gave them false identity papers and provided them with Swedish protection. Wallenberg, ironically, was later arrested by Soviet officers and disappeared in a Siberian prison camp. Thus, most of the Jews of Budapest—about 80,000—were spared, and they continue to be important in the city's, and Hungary's, life today.

BETWEEN WAR AND COMMUNISM

At the end of the war, Hungary once again found itself on the losing side, this time directly occupied by the victorious Soviet army. In October 1944, the Soviets set up a provisional government that heavily favored Communists, although the Populists and other parties were also included.

In the November 1945 elections, the Smallholders Party, representing the interests of small farmers and the middle class, won 60% of the vote, and the Communist Party received only 17%. The new government carried out a popular land reform program and began rebuilding the country. Although Soviet forces still occupied the country and shipped whole factories and other economic resources to the Soviet Union as "war reparations," Hungarians believed that they could maintain their independence and a democratic system.

But when tensions between the United States and the Soviet Union grew into the Cold War, the Soviets became determined to fully control the Eastern European political systems. Hungary's Communist leaders, eager for power, used Soviet pressure to squeeze out the other parties. These tactics included accusing opponents of being American spies and conspiring against Hungary. The leaders of the other parties, such as Prime Minister Ferenc Nagy of the Smallholders, were arrested or fled the country, and by 1948, the Communist Party was in full control.

During the Stalinist era, all houses (even those of the former upper class) suffered the indignity of having pictures of Stalin and Rákosi pasted on their front doors.

Since many of the fighters in the 1956 Revolution were teenagers, they could not legally be executed until the age of 18, so they were kept in prison for two years or longer and then executed when they came of age.

COMMUNIST HUNGARY

Hungary's Communist leaders, led by Mátyás Rákosi, forced a Stalinist system on Hungary. They outlawed all associations and organizations they did not control. They succeeded in rebuilding the country and developing heavy industry, transportation systems, and other modern improvements. But the result was a terrorized population, and prisons and labor camps filled with opponents and those whose family background was "suspicious."

In October 1956, declarations for reform by the Writers' Union and anti-government demonstrations by students led to a general uprising in Budapest. The rebellion spread throughout the country, and workers' councils took over the factories. Imre Nagy, a Communist who believed in a more human "Hungarian socialism," became prime minister and urged the rebel bands to lay down their arms, while trying to convince the Soviets that the situation could be resolved. Instead, the Soviet army invaded Hungary on November 4, crushing the rebellion.

The Soviets placed János Kádár in power in return for a promise to do their bidding. Hundreds of revolutionaries, demonstrators, and activists were executed. In all, about 20,000 Hungarians lost their lives and 200,000 left the country. Once again, Hungary lay devastated.

But Kádár was smart enough to know that the Stalinist era of total control of the people was over. He gave in to some of the demands of the revolution, such as ending the drive to collectivize agriculture, while condemning the uprising itself as a "counter-revolution" led by "fascists and spies." While remaining a loyal subject of the Soviet Union, Kádár was able to liberalize the economic system in Hungary, provide people with a better standard of living and privileges such as owning a car or a vacation house, and the right to travel to the West (unheard of in the other Communist countries), and gain some autonomy for his country.

Communist Hungary

By the 1980s, Hungary appeared very liberal—it was known as the "happiest barracks in the Communist concentration camp." Many goods were available and the people were freer to do and say as they pleased. But the Communist system still did not work very well, the political leadership was shortsighted and corrupt, and people were not really free.

After Soviet leader Mikhail Gorbachev began the changes in the Soviet system known as *glasnost* ("opening") and *perestroika* ("restructuring"), the leaders of the Eastern European countries, including Hungary, found it harder to resist similar changes themselves. Kádár was removed from power, and the new government agreed to enter negotiations with the opposition groups, which resulted in an agreement to hold free, multi-party elections in early 1990 and to move to a market economy and a free political system. Meanwhile, in 1989, Hungary decided to allow thousands of refugees from East Germany to pass unhindered across its border into Austria, thus playing a major role in the fall of the Berlin Wall and the "Iron Curtain."

In a symbolic gesture, Hungarians burn the portrait of Stalin to signify the end of the Communist era.

Hungary is now, after this century of great changes, to make perhaps the greatest changes ever in its political, economic, and social life. These changes are filled with difficulties and uncertainties, but Hungarians hope they will lead to a better future.

GOVERNMENT

HUNGARY IS IN THE MIDST of changing its political system from one where a single party, the Hungarian Socialist Workers Party, controlled every aspect of government to one in which different political parties, with different ideas and representing different constituencies, freely compete for the votes of the citizens. The first few years of this transition have not been easy. Even before the Communists took over, Hungary lagged far behind Western European countries in its political development. After 40 years of repressive Communist rule, people have gotten used to obeying their leaders, believing official lies, and voting when they were told. As a result, government in Hungary is in a state of flux, somewhere between Communism and real democracy. New laws and structures of government coexist with old habits and practices. Hungary is moving toward democracy, but when and whether it will arrive is an open question.

Opposite: **Seen from across the Danube, Parliament Building is imposing and dominates the horizon.**

Left: **The local town hall is the center of regional administration.**

THE DEVELOPING POLITICAL SYSTEM

Parliamentary delegates are elected in a complicated system involving both individual candidates and party lists (seats are allocated according to the support each party receives), as well as a "national list" meant to compensate for underrepresented parties.

On October 23, 1989, Acting President Mátyás Szurös proclaimed the beginning of the Hungarian Republic, replacing the People's Republic of Hungary. The change of name symbolized the creation of a completely new state, in which the rule of law would replace that of the Communist Party, the people would democratically choose their government, and individual rights would be protected. The Constitution of 1949 was amended at the same time, but the changes decreed by the still-Communist government were mostly cosmetic. The real changes—construction of a new voting system, judicial reforms, freeing of the media, and responsive and accountable government—have for the most part fallen victim to arguments in Parliament between the different parties. As a result, Hungarians are still waiting to see what their new government and political system will look like.

The new post-Communist Parliament was created as "the highest organ of state authority of the Republic of Hungary." Its 386 members, elected for four-year terms, are responsible for electing the president of the republic, the prime minister, and the members of the Constitutional Court, as well as approving the state budget and treaties, declaring war, and concluding peace. Parties must receive at least 4% of the vote to be represented in Parliament. The presidency is a largely ceremonial post, with certain important legal and constitutional functions, but real power rests with the prime minister and the ministers he or she chooses.

Hungary is divided into 24 counties and the metropolitan area of Budapest, below that into districts, and on the lowest level into communes, large communes, towns, and the districts of Budapest. The governing body for each of these levels has been changed from a Soviet-type council to a self-governing assembly of deputies. Local government is responsible for the administration of services, including education, health care, and welfare; the management of public property; collecting local taxes; and passing appropriate legislation.

Justice in Hungary is administered by the Supreme Court, the Budapest Metropolitan Court, and county and district courts. The Constitutional Court, whose members serve for nine-year terms, decides on constitutional questions. An important initial task of the judicial branch has been to decide how to deal with the many crimes—moral, political, and economic—committed by Communist officials over the past 40 years.

The new government has made progress on passing laws regulating the privatization of the economy, a new system of private property, and compensation for those who had property confiscated by the state. But other questions, such as ownership, control, and regulation of the media (especially radio and television) are still awaiting agreement by the main government and opposition parties.

Hungary's foreign policy has shifted from alliance with the Soviet Union firmly toward the West. Hungary is actively seeking full membership in the European Community and other European and regional common economic and political bodies.

Hungarians casting their vote in the 1990 elections, the first free multi-party elections in nearly half a century.

35

THE NEW PARTIES AND THEIR LEADERS

Hungary is currently governed by a coalition of center-right parties led by the Hungarian Democratic Forum (MDF by its Hungarian initials). MDF is a mixture of liberal and conservative politicians who share a concern for the Hungarian nation as a people in danger of losing its values and identity. The party favors privatization of the economy and a free market system. On social issues, MDF is generally conservative, glorifying the family and traditional values.

The party's leader until his death in December 1993 was József Antall. A conciliator by nature, Antall just managed to keep his ruling coalition together and the leaders are now struggling to keep their party from splitting. The pressures of many unsolved issues and of the difficult, divisive work of managing the transition have put great strains on MDF. In addition, as memory of the struggle against Communism fades, politicians are tending to divide into different factions supporting different interests.

The main opposition party is the Association of Free Democrats, or SZDSZ. Formed by the leaders of the "democratic opposition" movement of the 1980s, SZDSZ supports the fastest possible transition to a free market system, with complete freedom for investment by Western companies. In exchange for agreeing to support certain constitutional changes desired by MDF, SZDSZ was allowed to choose the president of the republic, playwright Árpád Göncz.

President Árpád Göncz was chosen on August 3, 1990, to the jubilation of his supporters.

THE PARTY OF YOUTH

"The future belongs to the young," the cliché goes, but in Hungarian politics the present too may soon be governed by young people. A party with, until recently, an upper age limit of 35 years for members, the Association of Young Democrats (FIDESZ) is the fifth largest party in the Hungarian Parliament. Recent opinion polls show FIDESZ is supported by over 25% of voters—more than twice the support of the ruling MDF—so it is quite likely that the youth party will be in a position to help

form the next government. Such a role for a party identified with the problems and hopes of young people is unprecedented in Europe. FIDESZ's young parliamentarians, who come to the solemn sessions in jeans or hot pants and boots, love to break traditional political molds. One of their leaders models for Levi's ads in his spare time, and their electoral campaign featured rock and pop music videos rather than the solemn political pronouncements of their opponents.

FIDESZ began as an alternative to KISZ, the Communist Youth League. Because they are young, FIDESZ leaders project an image of being "clean," innocent of the crimes of the system, and of representing a clear break with the past. The party's most visible leader, Viktor Orbán *(above)*, became known for his fiery speeches condemning the Communists for their lies and for depriving his generation of a future. A brilliant politician at the young age of 30, Orbán is now talked about as the possible next prime minister. FIDESZ is a strong voice in Parliament for a purely free market policy. The young politicians are seen to be firm and principled, but many Hungarians, especially older ones, have doubts about their ability to actually govern the country. The party has also been criticized for being a flashy image with no substance. Since it is very unlikely that any party will win a majority by itself, FIDESZ is now looking for other parties to form a coalition; SZDSZ and MDF are both possible candidates.

The former ruling party, the Hungarian Socialist Workers Party, renamed itself the Hungarian Socialist Party (MSZP). Its ideas are now practically in line with most of the West European socialist or social democratic parties. Despite the stigma of being connected to the former system, the parliamentary delegates of the MSZP are gaining respect as strong critics of the new injustices created by the transition.

LEARNING DEMOCRATIC VALUES

The Communist political system is gone, but "Communism in people's heads" remains. Hungary's 40 years of Communist indoctrination included the idea that society was constantly threatened by "enemies" both inside and outside, breeding distrust of one's neighbor and hostility to different views. The new politicians, although most were never themselves Communists, lived in the Communist system and are quick to accuse their opponents and try to exclude them from the debate.

Hungarian farmers, more conscious today of their rights and responsibilities, demonstrate for more government support for agriculture and farmers.

The two main parties, MDF and SZDSZ, after their initial agreement on nominating the president, fell to squabbling and attacking each other rather than working together to steer the country's historic transition. MDF has been accused of trying to control the media, similar to the Communists in the past. Opinion polls show public confidence in all of the parties dropping steadily; people believe that politicians on all sides are wasting time arguing with each other about trivial points rather than solving the pressing problems of the day. Turnout at elections has been surprisingly low, showing an increase in voter apathy and cynicism. Most experts feel that Hungary's democracy is on the road to stability, but some fear that a new kind of dictatorship, for instance a nationalist one, could replace the dictatorship of Communism. To prevent this, Hungarians need to take their rights and responsibilities as citizens of a democracy seriously, and the politicians must learn the skills to compromise and work together for the good of the whole country.

FROM OKTOGON TO NOVEMBER 7 SQUARE TO OKTOGON AGAIN

When they came to power after World War II, the Communists renamed streets, squares, and even whole towns to reflect famous names and dates in Communist history. Thus Oktogon (because of its eight-sided shape), a main square in Budapest, became November 7 Square, commemorating the date of the 1917 Russian Revolution. In the capital and in practically every town and village, streets and squares were named after Karl Marx, Friedrich Engels, Lenin, and other founders and leaders of Communism.

After the collapse of the Communist system in 1989, one of the first tasks of the new regime was to set about changing these hated reminders of the Communist era, usually back to their earlier names. Lenin Ring Road became Theresa Ring Road (after Empress Maria Theresa), People's Republic Avenue became Andrassy Avenue, Red Army Road became Üllői Road, and November 7 Square again became the Oktogon *(see above)*. With this step, planners and political leaders hoped to emphasize the end of Communist control over the social landscape and over the people themselves. So people could find their way around, the old street signs were left in place, with a red slash simply painted across them, and the new (or old) names put on new signs underneath the crossed-out ones. Bus and metro drivers announce stops by the new names now, but many people still refer to streets by the names they have known for years.

ECONOMY

AFTER OVER 40 YEARS OF COMMUNISM, Hungary's economy is now on the road to capitalism. The first few years of this unprecedented changeover have shown progress in many areas and the launching of thousands of new businesses and joint projects with Western investors. But the sharp rise in prices and growth in unemployment have left most Hungarians feeling economically worse than before, and fearing the future even more.

ECONOMIC INDICATORS

In 1992, Hungary's per capita income was $3,446. Although low by Western standards, this level is more than five times that of neighboring Romania. Hungary is generally poor in natural resources, with the exception of its abundant farmland and an estimated 10–12% of the world's reserves of bauxite. Other minerals are coal, found in substantial quantities but of low quality, and some uranium. Primary agricultural products are fruits and vegetables, grains, and livestock; major industrial products are buses, machinery, pharmaceuticals, and lighting equipment.

Main exports are agricultural products, bauxite, pharmaceuticals, and machine tools, while fuel, raw materials, semi-finished products, and light industrial goods constitute the main imports. Hungary's main trading partners are the former Soviet Union and the other East European countries as well as Austria, Germany, and the United States. In addition to an increasing trade deficit, Hungary's foreign debt now stands at $21.3 billion, the highest per capita in Eastern Europe.

Inflation seems to be slowing down, but remains high at around 25%. The unemployment rate was 13.3% at the beginning of 1993 and was expected to reach 20% by the end of the year, as more inefficient businesses close down. Western investment since 1989 is at $4.8 billion, the highest for any of the Eastern European "transitional" economies.

The Hungarian economy is still operating with outdated equipment. Both the carpenter (opposite) and farmer (above) would be more productive if they had access to modern machinery.

CREATING THE "SOCIALIST ORANGE"

Communist idealists believed that it was possible to grow or produce everything the country needed. Thus Hungary had to produce steel and grow cotton and oranges so as not to depend on capitalist countries. The campaign for the "socialist orange" was supposed to prove socialism was the superior system. But Hungary is not Florida, and it proved impossible to actually grow oranges there. Still, this failure could not be admitted without throwing the whole system into question, so "criminals" responsible for the failure were found and punished, and the efforts continued.

THE COMMUNIST LEGACY

The Communists had a grand vision for the peasant country: their goals were heavy industrialization, the creation of a large working class, and the collectivization of agriculture, turning farmers and farmhands into state employees. Under the principle that the country's resources belong to all the people, the state declared private ownership of land, shops, or factories illegal, and took away all property beyond personal belongings.

By the late 1960s, the Kádár regime realized that the only way to ensure a stable political system was to produce more consumer goods. The government allowed small private enterprises to be established, mostly shops, and later small restaurants and other food vendors appeared. In agriculture, members of state and collective farms were allowed to rent small plots to cultivate in their spare time and to keep the profits from their crops. The state was to concentrate on producing grain and livestock, which are more capital-intensive. As a result, food products became abundant, and consumer goods eventually became more plentiful as well.

As the control of the economy by Party officials and central planning offices decreased, more and more transactions and exchanges took place outside the official economy between private citizens and even between factories, collective farms, and enterprises. This whole network of trading and services became known as the "second economy," as opposed to the official or "first" economy.

However, the economy was in crisis. In the 1980s, the government instituted the first income tax in a socialist country. People were working harder and harder, yet their standard of living was falling.

*Appreciation money,
respect money,
hidden money,
handshake money,
honorarium,
spreading money,
sliding money.*

*—Hungarian
euphemisms for "bribe"*

STANDARD OF LIVING

The Communist system has left Hungarians with an infrastructure that is old, decaying, and substandard. Apartment complexes, buildings, factories, and streets are in disrepair or even falling apart. Equipment in manufacturing plants is outdated and inefficient.

One bright spot in this legacy is the public transportation system. Hungary is served by a solid network of trains and buses, so that even the smallest villages are reasonably accessible without a car. Transportation within cities and towns is also quite good (Budapest has the oldest subway on the European continent, dating from 1896). Public transportation in the past was subsidized by the government, but prices have been rising quickly in the new system and, though still cheap by Western standards, are a significant burden to Hungarians now.

Hungarians are hard-working, but have not been accustomed to putting that effort into their "regular" job. It is still hardly possible for many Hungarians, especially professionals and other "intellectual" workers in the state sector, to live on the salary from their primary job. Many must take on another job or freelance work, or do special projects to make ends meet.

Factory and manual workers begin work by 7:00 a.m. or earlier, and the official workday is over by 2:00 or 3:00 p.m. Offices start later, at 8:00 or even 9:00 a.m., but still usually close by 4:00 p.m. For all too many, the official "quitting time" is still seen as the time when "real" work, bringing in more money, begins.

Hungarian workers are hard-working and many take on second or third jobs in order to have a reasonable standard of living.

43

POLLUTION AND ENVIRONMENTAL DESTRUCTION

Hungary's water system has been contaminated by untreated sewage, runoff from fields treated with chemical fertilizers, and industrial waste. Fifty-four percent of Hungary's population lives without adequate sewage systems, and 773 towns and villages rely on unsanitary water supplies.

Air pollution, mainly from coal-burning power plants and cars, is also a major problem. Hungary ranks sixth in the world in per capita sulfur emissions, and sulfur is one of the worst air contaminants. As a result, 25–30% of Hungary's forests are affected by acid rain.

The land is threatened by increasing amounts of toxic and dangerous wastes. In the 1980s, Hungary was producing five million tons of hazardous wastes a year, as well as secretly importing wastes from Austria, Switzerland, and West Germany, in exchange for hard currency. Disposal was haphazard, much of it in illegal and unsealed landfills.

Sadly, many Hungarians give more priority to jobs and social welfare, and the Ministry of the Environment is given a very low budget.

The old mentality that nature and natural resources are to be exploited to the fullest still lingers in the minds of Hungarians. Dumps like this one are a familiar sight in industrial areas.

CREATING THE NEW ECONOMY

The road to a free market economy is very complicated and difficult. Many enterprises, including some of the biggest firms employing the most workers, are hopelessly inefficient and have attracted no private investors.

The few successes of the privatization program are the purchase of the light bulb manufacturer Tungsram by General Electric Corporation, the purchase of Duna Inter-

REVOLUTIONS IN RETAIL

The first McDonald's fast food restaurant opened in Budapest in 1988, soon followed by a small Adidas shop. Since 1989 Budapest, especially, has been swamped by American fast food outlets and other retail businesses, changing the way Hungarians consume.

There has also been a growth of individual vendors on streets and at the bazaar. Popular books, underwear, and other basic clothing are easily bought from a street vendor, who sets up a table or sells goods from a sports bag outside a subway station. For cheap shoes, imitation famous label clothing, and all sorts of odds and ends, the bazaar is the place.

This type of entrepreneurship takes advantage of the loosening of borders across the Eastern European region. Large numbers of Hungarians and citizens of many of the other former socialist states are making their living this way, traversing vast distances by car or train, sneaking goods through borders or paying off guards, buying at a low price and selling high.

continental hotel by the Marriott chain, investments totaling over $100 million by PepsiCo, and the opening of the first car manufacturing plant in Hungary by the Japanese company Suzuki. Some overseas Hungarians have also been active in promoting Hungary for Western investors.

But Western investment and aid has still not met Hungarians' great expectations, and new tariff barriers put up by the European Community against Eastern European products have put Hungarian exporters in a difficult position. Strong government spending on social programs to soften the impact of price rises has caused high taxes and large budget deficits.

By some measures, the prospects seem good: by 1991, there were some 318,000 private enterprises, of which 10,000 were foreign partnership ventures. But for most Hungarians, statistical success has a hollow ring. There is a widespread feeling that Western investors, former Communist enterprise managers, and the new "mafia" (Hungarian organized crime) have been the main beneficiaries. Steelworkers, miners, and other industrial workers, once laid off, have little hope of finding a job in a market requiring computer skills and the knowledge of English.

HUNGARIANS

HUNGARIANS SEE THEMSELVES as a small but unique people who have struggled for many centuries to survive in the midst of other, often hostile, nations. They have a strong sense of national and ethnic pride, and at the same time are often insecure about their future and place in the world.

The Carpathian Basin has long been a mixing bowl for many ethnic groups, and relations between Hungarians and the minorities living in the country have ranged from uneasy to hostile. Among Hungarians there is traditionally a strong division between city dwellers and country people. Sometimes they have less in common with each other than with people of other ethnic groups living in the same town or in a neighboring village.

Opposite: **Despite their harsh life, Hungarian women still retain an optimistic outlook.**

Left: **Two youngsters enjoy a ride on their grandfather's donkey.**

The aging population is becoming a heavy burden for the younger workers to bear.

POPULATION FACTS AND FIGURES

Hungary has a population of 10.3 million, of which over 90% are ethnic Magyars. Twenty percent live in Budapest, and another 42% in other cities and towns. The remainder live in rural areas, a relatively high percentage for Eastern Europe. Population density is 287 people per square mile, higher than the European average.

With a declining birth rate and lower life expectancy, Hungary's population has been getting smaller since 1981. The country now has the oldest population in Eastern Europe. But the life expectancy of Hungarians is also the lowest in Eastern Europe, brought down especially by high death rates (from overwork and stress) for working-age males.

Hungary's birth rate stood at 12.2 live births per 1,000 population in 1991. The number of abortions is high, at over 70% of the number of births. High rates of divorce and unstable family structures have also contributed to the lower birth rate.

About seven million ethnic Hungarians now live abroad. Most of them are in neighboring countries, many in Romania. Substantial numbers of Hungarians have also migrated to Western Europe, Australia, Canada, and the United States. Some 1.5 million Hungarians left for the United States between 1890 and 1910. Many Jews left the country during and after World War II, and over 200,000 Hungarians fled the Soviet occupation that crushed the uprising of 1956.

THE MAGYAR DISTINCTIVENESS

The Magyars took their name from one of the original seven tribes that settled in Hungary, the Megyers. Hungarians call themselves and their language "Magyar." The term *Magyar* is also used in English by social scientists to describe ethnic Hungarians, as opposed to the sum of all people living in Hungary. The word *Hungarian* comes from "Onogur," a Turkish or tribal word meaning 10 arrows, referring to the alliance of 10 tribes—later seven—that decided to unite and move west into Hungary.

Hungarians pride themselves on their pure and distinctive ethnic heritage. They are usually said to have "Asiatic" facial and physical characteristics, although there has been so much mixing of peoples since the arrival of the Magyar tribes that they are now not much different, in a racial sense, from the peoples around them. What is clear is that the main source of Hungarians' distinctiveness is the preservation of their language over the centuries. Hungarian is part of the Finno-Ugric family of languages, completely unrelated to any of the Slavic, Romance, or Germanic languages spoken in the surrounding regions. Hungarians see the preservation of their language and culture as a historic mission. St. Stephen's acceptance of Christianity and the later struggles against invading Mongols and Turks gave the Hungarians another mission, that of preserving Christianity and Western culture from, ironically, the "barbarians from the East," which the Magyars themselves had once been.

The debate among Hungarians over whether they are essentially "Eastern," and different from Europeans, or "Western," and fully a part of European culture and civilization, has become a major point of division in politics and culture. There is still no agreement over what it means to be Hungarian: nationalists accuse others of being "not Hungarian enough," and are in turn accused of being "not fully European."

"It can be said that Asia was the cradle of the Magyar, and this child of the East, who had been feeding on the breast of Asia for thousands of years, now came to learn in the schools of Europe."

—*Ferenc Jankovich, writer*

THE HUNGARIAN CHARACTER

The question of what is "Hungarian" was especially sensitive during the years of Communism, when Party activists tried to turn Hungarians into "Soviet people." Expressions of national or cultural pride were condemned as "nationalist deviation." During the pre-1989 Kádár era, it became more acceptable to explore the national character. But different groups defined a "good Hungarian" in different or even opposing ways, which often excluded other ethnic groups or political opponents from participating in the affairs of the nation.

Pride in being Hungarian leads to a great sensitivity about "losing face." Hungarians have never forgotten the instances of national humiliation—the 1526 defeat by the Turks, the defeat of the 1848 Revolution, or the partition of the country in 1920. And they are also very sensitive to everyday situations in which they might feel personally humiliated. The word *balek*

THE "MOST HUNGARIAN" HUNGARIANS

Hungarians have always felt an emotional connection with those people who were cut off from the country by the Trianon Treaty. This feeling was especially strong in the 1970s and 1980s, when there were reports of discrimination against Transylvanian Hungarians. Although Hungary was a less developed society, conditions for the outside Hungarians often remained even more simple and traditional.

Hungarians in Transylvania and elsewhere still live in ethnically uniform villages, practically cut off from the developments of the 20th century. They speak old forms of Hungarian and live simple, self-sufficient lives. These people are idealized by nationally-minded Hungarians as the "most Hungarian," in whom Hungarian culture can still be found in its "pure" form, unaffected by the consumer culture of the West. With Hungary becoming more integrated into Western Europe and a part of the international consumer market, many Hungarians are traveling to ethnic Hungarian villages in Transylvania to find their "roots." It is ironic that they feel they must go beyond Hungary's borders to find the real Hungary.

refers to someone who is cheated, and a *balek* often appears as the fool in Hungarian cartoons and television shows. Sometimes it seems that Hungarians are constantly watching out for people taking advantage of them, making them the *balek*. They have a sense of themselves as victims and feel that others, especially those from the West, can never understand them. Hungarians feel they have contributed to and sacrificed much for the West, but are not appreciated as full members of the European or Western community. Yet, they also are insecure about whether their run-down and inefficient society and their Hungarian mentality actually deserve to rank with the rest of Europe, and they are likely to contrast the poor service in a restaurant, unreasonable bureaucratic procedures, or a messy room with "the way they do things in Europe."

But Hungarians can also be very generous to foreigners. They possess an "old world" elegance and politeness, and will go out of their way to help a stranger. They are hard-working and full of ambition and creative energy. They can be exuberant celebrants and can also be deeply moved by compassion or the tragedy of fate.

Opposite: **Hungarians from Transylvania are supposed to be more genuinely Hungarian than even those living in Hungary.**

Despite the difficulties besetting the Hungarian economy, this Angolan father and his four sons have found a better life in Hungary.

MINORITIES IN HUNGARY

Germans, Serbs, Slovaks, and Romanians make up most of the recognized minorities in Hungary today. They speak Hungarian as well as their mother tongue—the latter very badly, for most of them. The minority groups have been offered generous civil rights, not least because the Hungarians want to set an example for their neighbors in treatment of the much larger Hungarian minorities across the borders.

Aside from the main recognized minorities, there are several thousand Greeks who received political asylum in Hungary after the 1968 right-wing military takeover in Greece, and smaller numbers of African, Arab, and Asian students and workers from small Communist countries who came to Hungary to study or work. A more recent phenomenon has been the arrival of large numbers of refugees from the turmoil in neighboring countries. Many of these are ethnic Hungarians, but they also include Romanians, Croatians, and, lately, large numbers of Bosnian Muslims from war-torn Bosnia-Herzegovina.

JEWS AND GYPSIES IN HUNGARY

More Jews—around 80,000—survived World War II in Hungary than in the other Eastern European countries, and many took up prominent positions in the postwar Communist government. This led many Hungarians to associate Jews with Communism, although most of the leading dissidents, or opponents of Communism, in the 1970s and 1980s were also of Jewish origin. Hungarians also remember the role that Jews played in the past: they formed a high proportion of the professional and merchant classes, filling positions that educated noble Hungarians thought were beneath them. Thus, ironically, there are Hungarian stereotypes of both the "Communist Jew" and of the "capitalist Jew." Now most Hungarian Jews are intellectuals and technical workers living in Budapest, are fully integrated into Hungarian social and political life, and feel as Hungarian as anyone. But old prejudices die hard, and anti-Semitism has reared its ugly head among the most extreme of Hungarian politicians since the fall of Communism.

The Gypsies *(right)*, or Rom as they prefer to be called, migrated to Europe from India during the Middle Ages. All European countries have a Gypsy population of some size, but the largest numbers are found in Eastern Europe. Hungary is home to some 500,000 Gypsies, by far the largest of the minorities. Gypsies originally made their living as peddlers, tinkers, musicians, and doing other door-to-door trades. Dramatic and romantic "Hungarian Gypsy music," such as *Piros rózsák beszélgetnek* ("Red Roses Are Talking"), is the traditional accompaniment to a Hungarian restaurant meal. Although this music has always been and is still played by Gypsy musicians, it is actually not Gypsy in origin, but a copy of 19th-century European café music.

After the industrialization and collectivization of Hungary, Gypsies were forced to settle down, respect borders, and be registered with the authorities. In exchange, they were provided with stable housing and jobs in factories or on agricultural cooperatives. But the prejudice that had dogged these darker-skinned people since their arrival in Europe remained, and they were kept in the lowest-paying, dirtiest, and toughest jobs. Hungary's Gypsies, along with those in other countries, are for the first time becoming aware of their cultural identity. They are organizing themselves into local, regional, and national associations and, through the SZDSZ party, have elected two delegates to Parliament, a first in Hungarian history.

SOCIAL DIVISIONS

After the Communist takeover, a substantial working class was created, made up of miners, steelworkers, bricklayers, machinists, and factory workers. Admission to high schools and universities, and positions in the Party and government administration were determined by social class, giving worker and peasant families an advantage and creating a kind of equality never seen before. Peasants were pushed into large collective farms, producing an "agricultural proletariat" or rural working class.

Beginning in the 1960s, a government concern with efficiency and production led to the creation of a class of technocrats, trained managers, engineers, and technicians who administered the factories and collective farms. At the same time, the nomenklatura, a class of officials in government and industry, took on more and more power at the local level and collected all possible privileges for itself.

A new middle class emerged in the 1970s and 1980s, when economic reforms allowed private farming as well as the operation of small private enterprises. After 1989, a free market gave a class of entrepreneurs and business people the chance to grow. The nomenklatura was able to transform itself from Communist officials into capitalist owners and managers, while keeping its ill-gotten wealth. The big losers in the transition are rural workers and blue-collar workers, whose factories are unprofitable and will likely have to close. The difficulties of changing the system have caused new social tensions and a growing gap between rich and poor.

One group that deserves special mention is the intellectuals, whose social and political role has been much larger in Eastern Europe than in the West. They have great ambition and creative energy that can help solve Hungary's problems, but they have always tended to speak for and about the masses of people without getting to know their feelings and desires.

Even though entrepreneurs and managers have been successful in the new economic order, the majority of the population still belongs to the working class.

GENIUS IN EXILE

Many Hungarians have made a name for themselves in the international arena. Unfortunately, most of them were living outside the country. Albert Szentgyörgyi discovered Vitamin C, found in especially high quantities in Hungarian paprika; János Irinyi invented matches; Oszkár Asbóth was the first to fly the helicopter over Budapest in 1928; Ányos Jedlik invented the electric motor, Otto Bláthy the electrical transformer, and Albert Fonó the jet engine; Dr. Ignác Semmelweis's proposal to sterilize all instruments used in childbirth caused an 80% drop in infant mortality.

In addition, Hungarians made discoveries that either laid the groundwork for or made possible the practical application of the phonograph (Farkas Kempelen's "speaking machine" paved the way for it); the telephone (Tivadar Puskás invented the telephone exchange, and established a "telephone newspaper"—the forerunner of today's electronic mail bulletin boards); the electric railway (Kálmán Kandó); and television (Mihály Dénes).

Baron Lóránd Eötvös revolutionized physics in the late 19th and early 20th centuries with his discoveries. He is remembered by several laws of physics and units of measure that are named after him, and Albert Einstein declared Eötvös's discoveries to be a pillar of his work. In the United States, János (John) von Neuman has been called "the father of the computer:" he directed the Electronics Computer Project at Princeton that developed the modern computer. Hungarians Leo Szilárd, Eugene Wigner, and Edward Teller made up half of the six-member team that directed the Manhattan Project, which created the atomic bomb for the United States during World War II. Teller later became head of the Livermore National Laboratory in California, and thought up the Star Wars nuclear defense program as well. In all, eight scientists of Hungarian origin won Nobel prizes for scientific research between 1905 and 1971.

Other Hungarians who emigrated to the United States in the last century made their names in non-scientific fields. Joseph Pulitzer *(right)* rose from a reporter for a German language newspaper in St. Louis to owner of the prominent *New York World,* funded the establishment of the Columbia Journalism School, made possible through donation the floodlighting of the Statue of Liberty, and is memorialized by the Pulitzer prize for outstanding writers, artists, and journalists. Ágoston Haraszty founded the California wine industry, importing 200,000 grape cuttings from Europe, including the famous Hungarian Tokay variety. Adolph Zukor produced the first American full-length film, *The Prisoner of Zenda,* and founded Paramount Pictures. William Fox founded the Fox Film Corporation, the forerunner of 20th Century-Fox movie studios.

LIFESTYLE

HUNGARIAN LIVING TODAY has been molded by the pressures of the past 40 years. Communism promised that people would have to work less, be healthier and happier, and live more comfortably. Instead, they had to work harder, live in small, run-down apartments, and spend most of their free time searching for basic necessities to make life livable.

URBAN LIFESTYLE

Hungarians in urban areas live in high-rise apartment complex developments called *lakótelep* ("LAH-koh-teh-lep"). These consist of dozens of ugly, uniform complexes towering 10 or more stories high and filled with cramped, identical apartments. These developments stand on the edge of towns and often require a long commute to the work place. But they include markets, shops, bars, and other amenities so that, except for work, it is not really necessary to leave the complex.

Apartments in the *lakótelep* consist of a tiny bedroom for the children that also serves as a study, and a slightly larger one for the parents that is also the living-and-dining room. The kitchen holds a stove and a fold-out table at which two can sit, and the bathroom is also tiny. Laundry is hung on the balcony or over the tub, and food, towels, kitchenware, and other necessities are stored in closets along the narrow hall.

Some older apartment buildings nearer the city centers have a more pleasant exterior, but the apartments are just as small and run-down. Fancier areas of town hold luxurious homes and villas previously occupied by Party officials. The worst type of accommodation are the "workers' hostels," usually decrepit dormitories for workers at large factories.

A new problem is that of homelessness. The *homelesszek* are now estimated at 30,000, and many of them line the major streets and subway stations of the capital, begging for spare change.

Opposite and above: **Apartment complexes everywhere in the country tend to be old and crumbling. However, there is such a shortage of housing that no one would even consider refusing an apartment just because it is in a run-down building.**

PLAYING THE APARTMENT GAME

The apartment complexes that ring the edges of all Hungarian and other Eastern European cities and towns are both the achievement and fiasco of the socialist system. Many Hungarians who moved to urban areas to fill the jobs created by industrialization were housed in them, and the monthly rent was just a few dollars. But there were never enough apartments to go around, and getting one's own apartment became one of every urban Hungarian's primary goals in life.

Although all housing was owned by the state, people were able to "buy" permanent rights to inhabit their apartments and, depending on their income, even to pass them on to children or grandchildren. Thus families registered a child at its grandparents' address in order to inherit that apartment when the child grew up; divorced couples were forced to continue living in the same apartment, and older couples lucky enough to each have an apartment avoided marrying to avoid giving one apartment back to the state. Young people, even if married, had to wait 10 years or more for their own apartment in the capital, and lived with their parents until then.

With the opening up of the housing market, now that state control is gone, there are more apartments available, but at exorbitant rents. A rush to build new single-family houses outside Budapest and other cities by newly wealthy entrepreneurs has also eased the situation somewhat. But for the majority of urban Hungarians who need the cheap, state-owned apartments, playing the "apartment game" will still be necessary for the near future.

The dream of every Hungarian is to have a weekend home where the family can relax.

GARDEN HOUSES

Middle-class Hungarians have been able to find relief from their cramped living conditions at "garden houses" or weekend retreats. The liberalizations of the Kádár government allowed families, after years of saving, to "buy" a narrow plot of land, usually a fraction of an acre, outside town. Great feats are needed to secure the necessary materials to build, with one's own hands, a tiny house, and families spend every weekend there, making improvements, cultivating fruits and vegetables, and even processing homegrown grapes into wine.

RURAL LIFESTYLE

In keeping with the sharp division between city and countryside, rural living is quite different from that of a *lakótelep* dweller. Hungarian peasants have come a long way since the 1930s; most now live in single-family homes, with a garden attached and a one-acre private plot of land some distance away. Most agricultural land is owned by the Tsz ("TAY-ess"), the Hungarian abbreviation for agricultural cooperative, which employs the peasants, but the land may soon be sold into private hands.

Peasants working after hours in their own gardens and on small private plots have for years produced more than half of Hungary's fruits and vegetables, and a substantial proportion of the livestock as well. Village dwellers are thus able to supply most of their own needs, and are envied by many city residents for what they see as the freer and more bountiful rural lifestyle. On the other hand, most villages lack the cultural and social amenities of the cities, and their social life may be restricted to men gathering to drink in the dark, smoky, and dirty *kocsma* ("KOHCH-mah") or bar.

Rural living can be harsh. However, as farmers and peasants grow their own food, they have more control over their lives than city dwellers and do not feel the stress of having to hold more than one job.

GIFTS, FAVORS, AND PATRONAGE

Since many things were not available for purchase during the Communist regime, people grew to rely on friends, relatives, and business associates to make ordinary transactions work. A construction worker might supply some building materials to a Russian teacher who would tutor his daughter in exchange. This system combined elements of a barter economy with the kind of kinship or patron-client relationship found in traditional societies. Sometimes transactions might involve three or four persons, or a favor might be repaid only many months later. But all Hungarians, from the lowliest laborer to the manager of a large factory, learned to be constantly on the lookout for people who could help them, and for ways in which they could assist others. They were always aware of debts and favors owed them in any social situation.

Although goods and services are freely available now, the "favor mentality" has remained strong with Hungarians. They tend to look for ways to beat the system, rather than attaining things directly. This characteristic helps knit people together in their interdependence on each other, but can also turn relations between people into a calculation of cost and benefit.

SOCIAL ATTITUDES

Although most Hungarians hated Communism and neither agreed with nor understood its ideology, the cradle-to-grave Communist welfare state has left a strong mark on Hungarian attitudes today. Hungarians have become accustomed to free health care, guaranteed jobs, and even vacations organized for them by their company or factory. Communist principles of equality for everyone, even if it meant everyone was equally poor and miserable, were internalized. Thus certain attitudes—such as the expectation that all of an individual's needs will be taken care of by the state and suspicion of anyone who is "doing better" than others—are deeply rooted, despite lip service paid to the Western values of individualism and free enterprise.

As a reaction to Communist attempts to regulate their lives, Hungarians are intensely protective of their privacy, are suspicious of highly organized group situations, and prefer to spend evenings at home with a few friends than go to a concert or nightclub. Hungarians mistrust authority and deride their leaders in private, but tend to obey laws and rules when they come up against them—another legacy of the harsh system in which even spitting on the sidewalk ("socialist property") could land them in prison.

CHILDREN, YOUTH, AND FAMILIES

Hungarian families have been getting smaller: the average is two children per family, and in the city one-child families are common. However, Hungarians maintain deep bonds with their families. They spend holidays together, send greetings for birthdays and name days, and keep in touch with all the relatives on a regular basis. Children rarely break off contact with parents. Even if family members are no longer on speaking terms, they usually keep informed about

Hungarian families are small, and parents take advantage of dinnertime as opportunities to impart their wisdom to their children. One of the values closest to the heart of the Hungarian is loyalty to one's family.

each other. Family members are expected to help each other out in getting around the obstacles of daily life and to drop everything to provide necessary assistance in a crisis.

Life for children and young people has not been easy. They generally spend many hours in day-care centers and nursery schools. Yet this pattern is changing, at least for affluent families. Hungarian children are dealt with quite strictly and are prepared for hard work and discipline later on. Young people do find time for pleasure, though, whether it is a soccer game in a vacant lot at dusk, a weekend of roughhousing at a crowded public swimming pool, or a romantic walk along the river.

Family life in the countryside is different. Families tend to be larger, and two or three children are the norm. Children spend more time with their families, helping out with chores around the house, in the garden, or in the fields. There is more room to move and relations are more relaxed.

FROM "YOUNG PIONEERS" TO "HUNGARIAN SCOUTS"

After the Communists took over Hungary, families were pressured to enroll their children in the "Young Pioneers," a kind of Communist Scout movement. The Pioneers were gathered together to meet government leaders and visiting dignitaries from other socialist countries and for parades on important Communist holidays. After "graduating" from the Pioneers, the next step was entering the Communist Youth League, or KISZ. Membership in KISZ was practically obligatory for young people who wanted to go to college or get job training. KISZ organized summer work camps, weekend outings, concerts, and lectures, but always with an eye to educating and forming young people to fit into the system.

The Association of Young Democrats, FIDESZ, began as an independent alternative to KISZ in colleges and high schools, before becoming a political movement, and finally a party. The Hungarian Scouts Movement *(above)* was also reorganized in 1989, carrying on the traditions of Hungarian Scouting from before World War II, and providing an organized alternative to the discredited Pioneers. Hungarian boys and girls now take part in group activities, such as hiking, swimming, and camping, to develop a sense of community, not just for the sake of conformity. The Hungarian Scouts have renewed their traditional ties with the Catholic Church, and boy and girl Scouts take part in processions and other religious activities.

However, some have charged that the new movement was designed to indoctrinate children with nationalist ideas in the same way that the Pioneers had done with Communist ideology. Most families simply prefer to let their children enjoy their leisure time without the supervision of an organization.

PRIDE AND PREJUDICE

Hungarians are extremely proud of their country and that they managed to preserve their traditions through centuries of war, revolution, and foreign domination. This national identity, while inspiring Hungarians to work together to create their new government and economy, has also given rise to a kind of dangerous nationalism that excludes and even victimizes those who are seen as "outsiders" or "enemies."

The Jews, who once controlled most of the businesses and commerce, have traditionally been the target of prejudice in Hungary. Anti-Semitism has reappeared, in graffiti against the opposition SZDSZ party, in desecrations of Jewish gravestones, and in the writings of populist writer István Csurka, who believes that Judaism is conspiring with the Americans, the Russians, and the International Monetary Fund to keep Hungary down. But Jews in Hungarian society are well established, very integrated, and able to defend themselves by political or legal means.

In Hungary, like in the rest of Europe, racism and bigotry are making a comeback, and skinhead youths have taken to attacking immigrants and anyone who looks different.

The group that increasingly has become the target of prejudice are the Gypsies, who are at the bottom of the social ladder and still lead a mostly separate life from the Magyar majority. They are being blamed for rising crime, violence, unemployment, and other problems that are new to Hungarians. Skinhead youths have taken to attacking Gypsies, along with African and Asian immigrants. People from the surrounding countries have also been victimized. This partly reflects old prejudices, but is also a reaction against forced Communist "solidarity" with other socialist states. Hungarians were forced to be good neighbors, but now that they are free, some would rather show their independence in a negative way.

BURDENS OF COMMUNISM: SOCIAL PROBLEMS

Hungarian authorities report that every year, between three and 10 people throw themselves in front of the train at Balatonszarszó, a small resort town on Lake Balaton. The great poet Attila József committed suicide in this fashion at the same spot in 1937, at the age of 32.

The continual struggles of the Communist years have left Hungarians in bad shape. Although Hungary, the "happiest little barracks in the Communist camp," appeared to be freer and more prosperous than its neighbors, the people paid a high price for their slightly better living standards. Most Hungarian men held two or even three jobs to make ends meet. Women worked full-time and kept the household together for their families, while making the extra effort required to obtain many basic necessities.

Hungarians were left with a crisis-ridden society. As a whole, they are in very poor health. The mortality rates for the population, especially for middle-aged men and infants, have risen substantially in the past 20 years. There are high rates of heart and circulatory diseases, cancer, and cirrhosis of the liver. The incidence of neuroses and other mental disorders is astoundingly high. In 1986, Hungary spent 3.3% of its budget on health care, one of the lowest percentages in Eastern Europe (in the United States the figure is over 20%). Considering the economic and budget difficulties of making the transition to a free market system, it is unlikely this figure will rise very much in the near future.

Hungarians try to compensate for their problems by drinking too much. Their consumption of hard liquor is the highest in the world, and they also consume beer and wine in great quantities. Almost 10% of males over 16 are officially classified as alcoholics; in the countryside, the rate is over 12% for all adults. Steady drinking, beginning in the morning, is a normal and accepted lifestyle for many. Bars open as early as 6:00 in the morning to accommodate this habit. The government made attempts to combat alcoholism in the 1980s by raising the prices of alcoholic beverages, but encountered little success. All of these problems have had their effect on the Hungarian family: they are unstable, and about 40% of all marriages end in divorce. Not surprisingly, Hungarians have the highest suicide rate in the world, almost 50 per 100,000 population per year—more than 1.5 times that of the next highest country, Denmark.

For most Hungarians, the harsh consequences of the transition to a new economic system have compounded the burdens of the past. Unemployment and inflation are rising very fast, an increasing portion of the population lives below the poverty line (estimates run between 25% and 40%), and, with the end of Communist discipline, rapidly rising crime rates make Hungarians more and more fearful. To these must be added the psychological effects of the abrupt and all-encompassing changes. Hungarians have lost the security of a restrictive but predictable system, without gaining the free and easy life they associate with the West. As a consequence they are confused and frustrated. They feel like they are experiencing the worst of both worlds: the backwardness and poverty of Communism, and the insecurity of life in the West. As the joke goes, "Hungary has now joined the world economy. We have a Swedish level of taxes with Ethiopian wages."

The rising cost of living has made life especially difficult for the older folk, some of whom have to resort to begging or playing the harmonica on the street to earn a few coins.

EDUCATION

Hungarian children enter elementary school at the age of six. In the first four years, pupils learn reading, writing, math, and basic science, as well as drawing and singing. In the next four years, subjects such as history, Hungarian language and literature, geography, individual sciences, and foreign languages are introduced.

High school students listen to their lecturer in front of the basilica during a field trip to Pécs.

After the eighth grade, the students in the top 20% can continue at the *gimnázium* ("GIM-nah-zee-uhm"), or academic high school. The next 25% go to a vocational high school, where they are trained for middle positions in industry, agriculture, trade, or health. Another 40% go to "skilled worker training schools." Closely tied to specific industries, these include on-the-job training. The rest join the work force. Less than half of the graduates from the *gimnázium* go on to the universities and colleges. Many people go to night school or take correspondence courses while working.

Hungary is now trying to reform its education system. These reforms include replacing the Communist-oriented view of history, politics, and philosophy with a neutral and Western-oriented one, and allowing the establishment of private schools and church-run schools. At the college level, reforms include doubling the student population by the year 2000 and consolidating the many different research institutes, universities, and technical and vocational colleges into six or eight university centers. This new system should operate more efficiently than the old one, although many academics and researchers may lose their jobs.

SEX ROLES AND WOMEN'S RIGHTS

In 1988, 82% of Hungarian women worked, a much higher figure than in Western countries. But leading positions in government and the economy were still held by men. Women earned 20–30% less than men for comparable work and often were segregated into highly-trained but low-paying positions in medicine and research.

The burden of Hungary's transition to a market economy is being borne disproportionately by women. They are the first to be laid off and fall more often into poverty than men do. The child-care system, which used to be free, is losing government funding and can no longer take care of everyone's children.

There is a conservative push to keep women out of the work force. Many Hungarians feel that Communism violated their traditional values by forcing women to work. So, among those families that can afford it, many women are now staying home to play a traditional role.

The darker side of the demise of Communist "official feminism" is the rise in prostitution and pornography. Many women find they can only meet rising costs by selling their bodies, and Budapest is becoming the Eastern European center for "sex tourism."

One issue that has brought Hungarian women together is the recent attempt by conservative and religious circles to restrict the right to abortion. Pressure from Hungarian women helped enact a new law that effectively leaves the decision completely up to the woman for the first 12 weeks of pregnancy.

During the Communist years, women had the opportunity to train in previously male-dominated technical fields.

RELIGION

HUNGARY'S CHRISTIAN ROOTS reach back nearly 1,000 years to the founding of the first Hungarian state and the crowning of King Stephen by the Pope. Since then, religion has been crucial in defining the Hungarian identity, and religious struggles have often been tied up with the struggles of Hungarians to survive. During the Communist era, state leaders promoted atheism as the official "religion," and churches, especially the predominating Catholic Church, suffered with the rest of society. As Communism faded in the 1980s, religion made a comeback as a symbol of anti-Communism and national identity, and church attendance increased. Hungarians today are curious about religion, but the church is not an important part of the life of most younger urban Hungarians. Among older people and in rural areas, the church still plays a strong role.

Roman Catholicism is still a driving force in the lives of older Hungarians, and St. Stephen is the focus of deep veneration. The relic of his right hand, usually housed in the Basilica of Esztergom *(opposite)*, is Hungary's holiest relic. On August 20, St. Stephen's Day, a grand procession goes through the streets of Budapest *(below)*.

RELIGION IN HISTORY

The Magyars brought their own well-developed pagan religious ideas with them into the Carpathian Basin. But King Stephen I realized that the adoption of Christianity was essential to the Magyars' long-term survival in Europe. When he chose Western (Roman Catholic) Christianity over the Eastern (Orthodox) variety, his decision put Hungary firmly in the West. Within a few years, Stephen succeeded in converting the whole country to Christianity, by force where necessary. Hungary's later participation in the European religious Crusades against the Turks sealed its Christian identity and commitment.

The Protestant movements against the Catholic Church during the Reformation quickly spread to Hungary. The Transylvanian princes who safeguarded some measure of Hungarian autonomy during the 150 years of partition between Turks and Habsburgs were mostly Protestants, and Protestantism became identified with the struggle for Hungarian independence against the super-loyal Catholic Habsburgs. Calvinism also became very strong in Hungary, and the eastern Hungarian town of Debrecen became known as the "Calvinist Rome," a center for that denomination of strict, ascetic Protestantism. When the Habsburgs got rid of the Turks and became sole rulers of Hungary, they used the Catholic Counter-Reformation movement—a Europe-wide counter-offensive against Protestants—to punish Hungarian desires for independence.

More than two centuries of Habsburg rule succeeded in turning Hungary into a primarily Catholic country. The attachment to the symbolic crown of St. Stephen proved stronger than opposition to the Habsburgs. The Catholic Church grew into a large landholder and one of the main pillars of economic and political power in the quasi-feudal system of the K.u.K. period (see page 25) and of post-World War I Hungary.

JEWS IN HUNGARY

The first Jews came to Hungary as servants of the original Magyar tribes. In the 16th century many Jews fleeing from Spain settled in Hungary, and later many more came from the Galicia region in southeastern Poland.

Hungary's Jews were divided into two groups. A very religious Orthodox population lived separately in its own communities, following very strict Jewish laws and practices. A less religious group lived in cities and towns, and took up important positions in the economy and later in society.

It was this latter group that most enthusiastically accepted the 19th-century proposition to "Magyarize" and became part of the Hungarian nation. Many of these secular (non-religious) Jews married non-Jews and even converted to Christianity themselves. If they made enough money, they could be accepted into the nobility, buy estates, and even become involved in the government, though they were still discriminated against socially.

The Holocaust in Hungary wiped out practically all of the Orthodox and rural Jewish communities. The remaining Jews, especially those living in Budapest, were already secularized. Today, these Jews value their Jewish heritage in a broad, cultural sense, and consider themselves Hungarians. They are more likely to celebrate Christmas than Hanukkah, and rarely go to a synagogue. There has been a recent resurgence of Orthodox Judaism in Hungary, which is a significant sign of the times, but it is not embraced by most Jewish Hungarians.

Hungary has the largest Jewish community in Eastern Europe, with between 90,000 and 150,000 practicing the faith.

Although the Communist regime introduced its own ceremonies to replace the Christian ones, people still went to church for baptisms, weddings, and funerals.

COMMUNIST ATHEISM

Communist ideology saw religion as a false promise of heavenly justice that could only lead the people away from the struggle for real Communist justice. In addition, the church in Hungary had been a firm supporter of the old order. Thus the existence of a strong church and widespread religious beliefs could not be allowed to exist under the Communist system. The Communists began by taking away the large landholdings of the Catholic Church. Party activists harassed priests and damaged churches, and the government directed a steady stream of propaganda against the Church. Cardinal Joseph Mindszenty, the highest Catholic official in Hungary, was imprisoned in 1949. He was released by rebels during the 1956 Revolution and took refuge in the American Embassy in Budapest, where he remained until his departure from Hungary in 1971, a lone symbol of opposition to Communism.

The Communists developed their own rites and ceremonies to replace those traditionally offered by the Church: a Pioneer initiation ceremony took the place of Baptism and First Communion, and a state ceremony was required for all marriages. A Communist funeral ceremony was also developed, though it was not forced on people and it never caught on. Especially after the Stalinist era, when the campaign against the Church was relaxed, Hungarians resumed baptisms and church marriages (in addition to the civil wedding). The churches reached an accommodation with the Communist rulers, in which they were allowed to operate without harassment and even received a certain amount of state support, in exchange for accepting the supreme authority of the Party and the permanency of the Communist system. But, by this time, Hungarians, not the most religious people in the first place, had lost interest in religion, and church attendance never rose beyond a small portion of the population.

WITH OR WITHOUT THE CROSS

One of the first items of debate for the new freely elected Parliament in 1990 was the restoration of Hungary's traditional coat-of-arms. This national symbol—called a *címer* ("TSEE-mehr") in Hungarian—was established in its present form by Lajos Kossuth during the 1848 Revolution and worn illegally on national day protests against the Communist regime. Alternating red and silver stripes make up the left side, while the right side contains a silver patriarchal cross coming out of a gold coronet on a green field. The whole is topped by the crown of St. Stephen.

But one sticky point quickly became apparent and led to days of heated debate in Parliament and in the media: many delegates saw the introduction of a national symbol with a cross as a violation of Western liberal democracy, a fundamental part of which is the separation of church and state. They also felt that this official symbol threatened the principle of tolerance toward non-Christian religions. The opposition proposed that the Kossuth *címer* be adopted without the cross.

After a long debate, the supporters of the cross won the vote by a narrow margin. This victory encouraged those who feel that Christianity is essential to Hungarian identity to propose the introduction of religious education in all public schools, an idea that was also strongly opposed.

RELIGIOUS REVIVAL AND NATIONAL IDENTITY

As the Communist system fell apart in the 1980s, people turned to the church for new ideas. But because of the willingness of Hungarian church authorities in the past to compromise with the Communists, the church in Hungary received much less respect and played a much smaller role in the breakdown of the Communist system than in Poland, East Germany, or Czechoslovakia.

Where religion did play a big role, and continues to do so, is on the symbolic level. The Christian religion has long been tied to the idea of Hungarian national independence through the Holy Crown of St. Stephen. So the crosses that many young people wore in the late 1980s symbolized not only the rejection of Communist

RELIGIOUS AFFILIATIONS

Roman Catholics	(estimated) 7,000,000
Calvinists	1,900,000
Lutherans	430,000
Jews	90–100,000
Orthodox Christians	35,000
Jehovah's Witnesses	27,000
Buddhists	3–4,000
Muslims	3,000
Hare Krishnas	1,500
Others	120,000
Unaffiliated	5–700,000

atheism, but also loyalty to the Hungarian nation and its independence. The MDF party successfully used religious symbolism to present itself as the truest representative of Hungarian values and win the 1990 elections.

Surveys show that nearly half of all Hungarians today are "interested" in pursuing religious ideas, though a much lower number are actually affiliated with a church. The Catholic Church is opening new schools, as well as seminaries and religious orders, and has applied for the return of its confiscated property. But even the renovation of the few buildings that have been returned so far is straining the Church's resources, and it is doubtful that the larger plans can be carried out completely.

Hungary now officially recognizes 36 different religions, meaning that they get a level of state funding based on their size. These include, in addition to the main religions (Catholic, Calvinist, Lutheran, and Jewish), religions not traditionally found in Hungary, such as Buddhism and Islam. Four religious groups, including the Jehovah's Witnesses and the Hare Krishnas, are excluded because they are considered "socially destructive," and are accused of separating young people from their families. The new interest in all things foreign has brought a number of more unusual religions to Hungary, including the Krishnas, the Pentecostals, and a number of fundamentalist missionary groups. Obscure Protestant sects draw thousands to revival meetings. Hungarians will continue to experiment with offbeat religions, as with other trends, until they tire of their new freedom to do so.

Although Christianity (opposite) **is still the main religion, several new religious groups have begun to appear on the streets of Budapest, including the Hare Krishnas** (below).

LANGUAGE

THE HUNGARIAN LANGUAGE is unique and sounds strange to the untrained ear. Hungarians are proud of the uniqueness of their language, and it forms a major part of their identity. Hungarian is difficult to learn, and few foreigners make the effort, so Hungarians have always had to use other languages—Latin, German, Russian, and English—to communicate with the outside world.

THE UNIQUE MAGYAR TONGUE

The original language brought by the Magyar tribes was influenced by the Turkic language spoken by the tribes that conquered them, and much later by the Turkish Ottoman Empire that ruled most of Hungary in the 16th and 17th centuries. Several hundred words, mostly related to farming, were borrowed from the agricultural Slavic tribes that the Magyars themselves conquered when they occupied the Carpathian Basin. Further influences were provided later by Slovakian, Serbian, and the other surrounding Slavic languages, as well as by Latin, French, and—on the force of the several hundred years of domination by the Austrian Habsburg Empire—German. But despite all of these pressures and influences, the basic character of the Hungarian language remained unique and unchanged. Hungarian today is a linguistic island: a language of Asian origin molded by European history.

Opposite: **A folk saying goes: "Who speaks Hungarian? The Hungarians and God Almighty." Due to the difficulty of their own language, most people in Hungary have learned to speak a second language. In the picture, a notice indicates the sale of German magazines.**

HUNGARIAN CONTRIBUTIONS TO ENGLISH

Hungarians pride themselves on their language's contributions to English. These include *coach* (in the more commonly British sense of bus or carriage) from the Hungarian *kocsi* ("KOH-chee"), or vehicle; *dollar*, from *tallér* ("TAH-lair"), the old Hungarian word for gold coins; and, most clearly, *itsy-bitsy*, from the expression *ici-pici* ("IT-see PIT-see"), meaning very little.

Having a chat on a park
bench by the lake: what
can be more romantic?

THE CHARACTER OF THE LANGUAGE

Hungarian is an "agglutinative" language, meaning that easily recognizable word stems are expanded by adding prefixes and suffixes to create expressive compound words. There are no pronouns in Hungarian; relations like *in*, *on*, *at*, and *around* are expressed by suffixes, as are possession and the identity of the subject, or the object of the sentence.

Another confusing aspect is word order: Hungarians tend to start their sentences with the things they feel need to be emphasized most at that particular moment. This is very flexible. It is as if the sentence "John gave Mary the cat" could just as well be "John the cat gave Mary," or even "Gave John Mary the cat." Hungarians know whether a word is a subject or an object by its suffix, not by its place in the sentence.

The Hungarian language also makes no distinction between male and female: the pronoun *ő* stands for *he*, *she*, and *it*. But this does not mean that Hungarian is less "sexist" than other languages—any woman holding an occupation or position must be identified by adding *nő* (woman) to the title (e.g. *tanárnő*, from *tanár* and *nő*, teacher-woman).

THE LANGUAGE OF MANY VOWELS

The Hungarian language has more vowels than almost any other—14 in all. These consist of seven "short" vowels, *a, e, i, o, u, ö, ü,* and their long forms *á, é, í, ó, ú, ő,* and *ű.* What looks like an accent mark, however, does not denote syllable stress or a slightly altered pronunciation like in French or Spanish, but is in fact a completely different letter. The long *á,* for example, is listed separately in the dictionary from *a,* and pronouncing or writing one instead of the other

is likely to create a completely different word. This is one thing that makes Hungarian especially hard for foreigners, since mispronouncing or switching a short vowel with a long one will result in a blank stare from a Hungarian. What sounds like a minor shift to a foreigner is, to a native speaker, a completely different sound, and therefore word.

LANGUAGE AND NATIONALITY

In the early 19th century, a developing class of intellectuals made writing and speaking in Hungarian a national campaign, and Count István Széchenyi shocked the Budapest Parliament by speaking Hungarian to the delegates, instead of Latin. The joint efforts of poets and politicians by the late 19th century established Hungarian as the dominant language.

The Hungarian language became the definer of Hungarian nationality. In order to secure a Hungarian majority in the territory, Hungarian nationality was offered to anyone who would adopt the language. Thus, to this day, a "true Hungarian" is defined in terms of allegiance to the Magyar tongue as one's first and primary language. Hungarians tend to be very concerned that their language be spoken and written "correctly."

Hungarian is standardized. There are no major dialects and little regional variation. Hungarians living in a Transylvanian village may speak an "older" form of Hungarian, but it will still be immediately understood by someone from Budapest. There is some difference between the Hungarian spoken in villages and that spoken by city dwellers, but this is more the result of education than of variation in the language itself.

The Hungarian nobility preferred to speak Latin, German, or French. Many had only a crude or no knowledge of their native tongue.

Hungarian names are said "backward," with the family name first and the Christian name second. Thus the great composer is really called Bartók Béla, and the former prime minister Antall József. A formal title comes at the very end: Dr. John Smith would thus be Smith John Doktor (or, to be very formal, Doktor úr). Foreign names are generally spoken in the "normal," Western order.

GREETINGS

Hungarians are very formal and proper in their relations with each other. In pre-Communist times, numerous titles and corresponding forms of address were used to define exactly the ranking of all of society, from the king right down to the lowliest peasant serf. During the Communist period, the old forms of address were abolished in favor of the universal *elvtárs* ("EHLV-tarsh"), or comrade.

Hungarians address any adult by the formal *ön,* until or unless invited to use the informal *te.* But neighbors will often use the formal form with each other for years. Married people generally address their in-laws formally for the rest of their lives. Younger adults are less formal with each other, and tend to use the *te* form without hesitation. But when in doubt, Hungarians always choose the formal version, to avoid embarrassment or insult. An older form of the formal address, *maga* ("MAH-gah"), can sometimes be heard, but it is also used as an insult.

MINORITY LANGUAGES

Although there are educational opportunities available in minority languages (German, Slovakian, and Romanian), members of these groups often speak Hungarian better than they do their "native" tongue. Still, street and shop signs are found in these second languages in villages that have a large proportion of minorities living in them.

Those most likely to speak Hungarian poorly are the Gypsies. More than half speak Hungarian as their native language, but substantial numbers speak only the Gypsy language, Romany (a relative of ancient Sanskrit, brought from the Gypsies' original home, which was India), and Romanian. This circumstance divides the Gypsies and alienates them still further from the mainstream.

FROM RUSSIAN TO ENGLISH

During the Communist period, the learning of the Russian language was made compulsory for all Hungarian schoolchildren from the fifth grade onward. A student who went on to high school would end up having "studied" Russian for eight years or more, but he or she was proud to have forgotten most of the language of the Soviet occupiers within a few short years after leaving school. In 1990, the new government abolished the compulsory study of Russian in schools, and now students may choose any of a number of Western languages instead.

Hungarians are now eager to learn Western European languages, especially English and German. Knowledge of these two languages will help them do business in the international arena and adapt to Western culture. Private language schools, with names like "London Language Studio" or "Boston Language School," have sprung up all over the capital and can be found in many smaller towns as well. Many young Hungarians can speak English, and are eager to practice the language whenever they get the opportunity. Older people are more likely to know German. If you know Russian, you might still be able to converse with one or two former high officials or the rare lover of Russian culture.

Posters targeted at trendy young people are now as likely to be written in English or German as in Hungarian.

ARTS

THE ARTS IN HUNGARY have a long tradition of confronting the country's two constant problems: the lack of national independence and the absence of social justice. For centuries, the arts—especially literature— have played a major role in social movements and, at key points in Hungarian history, have been the spark that set off revolutions.

The transition to a free market system has brought sudden changes that have proved very confusing to Hungarian artists. State subsidies are being cut drastically, and artists, musicians, and writers must quickly learn how to be commercially successful in order to survive. At the same time, the fall of Communism has deprived creative artists of a target for their protests and satirizations. Without state funding, the arts in Hungary today are in a financial and creative crisis.

Opposite and below: **The change to a free market economy has resulted in a proliferation of street artists and musicians. They now have to learn how to make a living from their artistic talent.**

LITERATURE AND THE NATION

The best-known examples of early Hungarian literature are the *Gesta Hungarorum*—chronicles of a monk, known only as "Anonymus," which told the story of the Magyars' migration, settlement, and development up to around A.D. 1200—along with the work of the first great Hungarian poet, Janus Pannonius, the star of King Matthias Corvinus's 15th-century court.

Hungarians are avid readers and the bookseller's kiosk is a familiar sight on Budapest street-corners.

The first major poet to write verse in Hungarian instead of Latin was Bálint Balassi, who started a tradition of lyric poetry in the 16th century. He died defending the holy city of Esztergom from the Turks. In occupied Hungary during the 16th and 17th centuries, poets kept the nation's spirit alive by bringing news from fortress to fortress.

The two centuries of Habsburg rule were a setback for Hungarian literature, because educated Hungarians then spent most of their time abroad. But the proposal by Habsburg Emperor Joseph I, in 1784, to make German the official language of the nation, spurred a new wave of literary rebellion. Writers such as Ferenc Kazinczy, who rejuvenated the language with modern words, József Katona, whose *Bánk Bán* (Regent Bank) qualifies as the first great Hungarian drama, and poet Ferenc Kölcsey, whose *Himnusz* (Hymn) became the Hungarian national anthem, all focused on improving and glorifying the Hungarian language in the service of national unity. The Revolutionary Era of 1848 produced Hungary's most beloved poet, Sándor Petőfi.

INNOVATION AND CONFLICT

The 20th century saw a new phase in Hungarian writing with Endre Ady's *New Poems*. He combined modernist ideas with traditional national values. The result was a strange yet beautiful style of writing and controversial ideas on politics, that opposed war and the oppression of peasants.

Writers flocked to Paris and other European capitals to sample the new, avant-garde creative movements of impressionism, expressionism, modernism, and (later) dadaism. The literary focus shifted from traditional settings in the countryside to Budapest. Alongside the old Hungarian literature grew a new, cosmopolitan style befitting a modern European capital. The flagship of this new style was the journal *Nyugat*, begun in 1908, which was a potpourri of poetry, short stories, novels in serial form, essays, news reporting, political commentary, and translations of foreign literature.

After World War I, a group of young writers and students began going out to the countryside, exploring conditions there and looking for "the real Hungary." What they found was appalling poverty. Out of this "village explorers movement" came the populist movement, which has remained a major force in Hungarian literature to this day. Gyula Illyés produced probably the finest example of these writings, *People of the Puszta*.

The populists' city counterparts were the urbanists. These were the cosmopolitan writers of Budapest, who took the city and the whole world as their subject, and who grouped around the *Nyugat* and other journals. The journals of the 1930s were filled with bitter debates between the populists and the urbanists, on both literary and political topics. One urbanist who achieved immortality in Hungarian literature was the tragic poet Attila József. He was born in a poor rural settlement and orphaned at a young age. A self-educated man, he worked at all sorts of odd jobs and wrote brilliant, tortured, rhyming verses.

The writers of the interwar era did much of their work—and carried on most of their debates—in Budapest coffee houses, mostly in the Café New York. This continued a long tradition—Sándor Petőfi had, after all, proclaimed his 1848 revolutionary demands in such a café. After the fall of Communism, the New York, which had been renamed the Hungaria, regained its old name and again became a center for literary life—as well as a tourist attraction for intellectuals.

TIVADAR CSONTVÁRY-KOSZTKA AND HUNGARIAN PAINTING

Hungarian painting has been much less important for the development of the nation than literature, and has gained much less international recognition than Hungary's musicians and composers. Hungary's history of foreign occupation made it difficult for artists to find the support they needed to develop a characteristic national style. When a demand arose for paintings in the 19th century, Hungarian artists did little more than imitate the styles current in Vienna or France, especially classicism. At most, they took Hungarian historical events or personalities for their subjects. Mihály Munkácsy was probably the most renowned of these 19th-century painters, although he spent most of his creative life in Paris. The prolific post-expressionist painting of József Rippl-Rónai at the end of the last century brought Hungarian art up to the most advanced current styles.

In 1881, a young pharmacist in the southern Hungarian town of Pécs experienced a vision. God appeared before him and told him to go to the ends of the earth and paint the spiritual wonders he saw. Tivadar Csontváry-Kosztka set off to fulfill this destiny. The paintings he produced in the next few years show mystical and religious subjects *(above, Mary's Well in Nazareth)*, strange and symbolic figures, and seductive colors, often painted on huge canvasses. Csontváry painted wondrous scenes from Sicily, Lebanon, Jerusalem, Switzerland, and the Hungarian *puszta*. His paintings all exhibit the painful gap between his mad, holy visions and the desolate reality of human life that he saw. Although his work has been classified as expressionist, it shows signs of primitivism and naturalism, and even of the future trends of art nouveau and surrealism.

Csontváry's genius was little recognized during his wandering lifetime. He was "discovered" in the 1920s, after his death, and again in the 1950s. In recent years, his paintings have become extremely popular among younger Hungarians. Prints of Csontváry's paintings, like *Solitary White Cedar* or *Pilgrimage to the Cedars of Lebanon*, gracing the wall of a Hungarian *lakótelep* apartment, represent the romantic hopes and often difficult reality felt by such apartment dwellers today.

FROM LISZT TO LIGETI

Hungarian music is a product of two traditions: the mainstream classical European tradition, and a unique, "Asian" type of native music. The Rákóczy Rebellion of the 18th century generated a characteristic form, the *kuruc* song, which was passed on from one generation to the next.

Hungary's contribution to classical music was the work of pianist and composer Franz Liszt. Born in 1811 of a Hungarian father and an Austrian mother, he strove to "work for the development of Hungary's musical culture." Although he got his musical education in Vienna and spent much time in Germany and Italy, Liszt consistently used Hungarian themes, both musical and historical, in his compositions.

Zoltán Kodály and Béla Bartók were heirs of Liszt's legacy. Kodály, Hungary's favorite composer, devoted himself to general music education. His persistent advocacy of making music available to all helped spread an appreciation of music to all Hungarians. Since Kodály, Hungarian music has been characterized by competent and prolific productions of standard classical works, based around such institutions as the Music Academy, the Budapest Philharmonic, the Hungarian Radio Choir, and the Franz Liszt Chamber Orchestra. The isolation of the Stalinist years and the general discouragement of innovation have caused the greatest names in Hungarian music since Kodály, such as György Ligeti, to emigrate and make their careers elsewhere.

It is fitting that this school choir should perform in front of a portrait of Zoltán Kodály, a man who devoted himself to the musical education of Hungarians.

BÉLA BARTÓK, A HUNGARIAN ORIGINAL

Classical and modernist composer Béla Bartók, together with his colleague Zoltán Kodály, spent his summers traveling to small villages and rural settlements to collect samples of genuine folk melodies. They asked village elders to sing the songs they remembered, and recorded the results on wax cylinders. Their efforts saved the vanishing native musical traditions. Today, over 100,000 different recordings are classified and preserved in the archives of the Hungarian Academy of Sciences.

Bartók, like Kodály, saw native melodies as the deepest expression of the "true Hungarian soul." He incorporated his Hungarian collections—as well as those he made of the melodies of neighboring Slovakians, Romanians, Bulgarians, and Turks—into his compositions, which ranged from folk songs to dissonant modernist experiments. Unlike Kodály's, Bartók's music never became a favorite of Hungarian listeners; it is often difficult and strange. But pieces such as his *Microcosmos* for the piano, his piano quartets, and his later *Concerto for Orchestra* are considered masterpieces of precision, innovation, and individuality. Bartók died in exile in New York in 1945, poor and lonely.

Bartók's role in Hungarian culture did not end with his death. His music was banned in Hungary during the 1950s, and young people played his records as an act of political opposition. Later, in the 1970s, his name came into use by populists as an adjective expressing pure interest in peasant art: as in a *bartóki* person, or even *bartókiság*, "Bartók-ness." His memory was rehabilitated by the reform-minded late Kádár regime. His portrait was put on the 1,000-forint note, and one of the three state radio stations is called Bartók Radio (the other two are named after Lajos Kossuth and Sándor Petőfi)—elevating him to equal status with the greatest national heroes.

In 1988, negotiations between the Hungarian government and Bartók's two sons resulted in the return of his remains to Budapest for reburial. The body was brought by ship from New York to England and then by motorcade across France, Germany, and Austria, with concerts at major towns along the way. The event dominated the Hungarian media for weeks, and the essentially apolitical composer was celebrated all at once as a populist, an urbanist, an anti-fascist, an advocate for minority rights, a national hero—and, almost as an afterthought, as a musician.

COMMUNISM AND CULTURE

The arts in Hungary in the early 1950s were dominated by "socialist realism," meaning that all art had to reflect the reality of the "socialist person." Short stories and novels told of workers or peasants overcoming doubts and learning to work harder for Communism, eventually joining the Party and vowing to work even harder in the future. Paintings and sculpture likewise turned to depictions of strong, self-sacrificing, heroic workers holding the Communist flag high. Even in poetry and music, odes to Soviet leader Joseph Stalin, or to Hungarian leader Rákosi, were preferred. Some writers were able to preserve their integrity by writing "for the desk drawer"—works that could not possibly be published at the time, but that might be able to appear in the future if the system ever changed.

The Kádár era was one of compromise and liberalization. Much more was allowed to be published, produced, and shown than previously, although there were certain very firm limits. No criticism of the Soviet Union or the Soviet-Hungarian alliance was allowed, nor of the socialist system or of the leading role of the Communist Party in political life. Private matters, such as love, death, and family life, were free territory, and social problems could even be brought up if done carefully. Writers learned the limits of what was allowed and began to restrain themselves to avoid the risk of crossing the line and being persecuted.

The 1960s and 1970s produced a new wave of art, exploring the conditions of life for the majority of Hungarians. Prominent examples were studies by György Konrád, a sociologist who later became a novelist and political essayist, and by Miklós Haraszti, a dissident activist now a member of Parliament for the opposition SZDSZ. There was a blossoming of novels, short stories, poetry, and all other kinds of writing, on themes personal and historical, and sometimes somewhat political.

A love poem was allowed to be published only if the hero discovered that the struggle for Communism was more important than personal happiness.

89

"READING BETWEEN THE LINES"

Communist rulers tried to control the cultural arena through an extensive and thorough system of censorship that was firmly established by the beginning of the 1950s. All newspapers, magazines, articles, books, plays, films, works of art, and even songs had to be approved by Party authorities before they could be presented to the public. To pass censorship, the work had to have a Communist political view, fit the form prescribed by socialist realism, and not offend any powerful leaders. Artistic and political persons who fell out of grace became "non-persons," and could not be referred to by anyone by name.

This system of censorship softened in Hungary during the Kádár era, and by the late 1960s, there was no longer any pre-screening of written work. (Theater, film, and music still had to be approved in advance.) But direct opposition to the system was still not permitted, and it was left to editors to be responsible for the invisible lines that should not be crossed, or risk losing their jobs. Writers especially, and other artists too, developed a sense of what they could safely write and produce, and what would go too far—in short, they became their own censors.

One way to avoid the problem of self-censorship was a style of allegory that became known as "reading between the lines." Creative artists adopting this style used a seemingly innocent setting—an incident from the past, from another country, or both—in such a way that a clever reader or audience knew that the moral or political lesson of the work was to be applied to the current situation in Hungary. The Revolution of 1848 was a favorite early subject, allowing writers such as Gyula Illyés to indirectly advocate a fight for national independence. Later, the soccer field became a common setting; Miklós Mészöly's *Death of an Athlete* caused a scandal, and Antal Végh's story, *Why is Hungarian Soccer Sick?* was actually withdrawn from the market within days of its appearance—apparently the lines to be read between were a little too wide. Géza Ottlik's *School on the Border,* set in a pre-World War II military school, showed the ominous effects of the over-disciplining of youth; others used insane asylums or other institutions to spin dramas of the individual's relationship to society.

Hungarian theater was subject to the strictest control from the very beginning of the Communist era, because of the theater's potential for subversion. But hard as it tried, the state was unable to ensure that socialist realism ruled the stage, and plays in particular were used to transmit hidden political messages. Such details as the scenery or costuming of a familiar and seemingly safe work could tip the audience off that another meaning was intended. Thus the staging of Shakespeare's *Hamlet* caused a major scandal in 1952—and a lesser one some 10 years later, as the director subtly but unmistakably referred back to the earlier scandal. László Németh's 1953 play, *Galilei* (about the late Renaissance Italian scientist), was performed for the first time just days before the outbreak of the 1956 Revolution, contributing to the upheaval. Clever artists and audiences found that even works by genuine Communists like the German playwright Bertolt Brecht could be turned against the corrupt Communists of the Kádár era.

THE FILM INDUSTRY

After 1958, the Hungarian film industry was reorganized and, surprisingly, given a large amount of freedom to explore new and critical themes. Miklós Jancsó, one of Hungary's greatest directors, made *The Hopeless* in 1965, about Hungarian peasants forced to act as collaborators and traitors during the 1848 Revolution, a theme that paralleled the humiliation of the peasantry in the 1950s. The Stalinist years became a frequent topic, whether of critical dramas, cutting farces, or hard-hitting documentaries.

Márta Mészáros is a fine director who deserves greater international recognition.

István Szabó, Hungary's most prominent director, used the financial plight of the state studios in the 1980s to his advantage. Hungarian studios were forced to enter into co-production agreements with West European studios, and a director as famous and brilliant as Szabó could use this situation to make films that were both seen by international audiences and implicitly critical of his country's political system. An example is *Mephisto*, about a German artist who sells his soul to the Nazis; the film is easily understood as a parable about the compromises made by his fellow Hungarian artists under Kádár. A distinction of the Hungarian film industry is the prominent role of women directors, of whom Márta Mészáros is the best-known, in making documentaries and dramas that deal especially with the problems of women in Hungarian society.

Hungarian pop music is becoming more negative and destructive as young people lose all hope of connecting with society.

FROM POP TO PROTEST

The first rock music in Hungary came in the early 1960s, as more or less a direct import from the West, but translated into Hungarian. Lyrics tended toward standard love themes, although a few songs touching on politics or human rights were banned.

By the late 1970s, new influences were reaching Hungary from the West, in the form of reggae, punk, rap, and heavy metal. The same problems that fostered these movements in the West—inflation, poor employment prospects, housing shortages, and general alienation from society—showed up in Hungary too, only coupled with a more intense hopelessness. There was consequently an explosion of new groups and their music, which was angry, outrageous, and opposed to the system.

Some of the groups tried experimental forms. But others adopted sexist, racist (anti-Gypsy or anti-immigrant), or even fascist/Nazi themes, using extremely violent and profane language and images in their songs and performances. Their popularity has continued to grow, expressing the radical mood of some young people in the country.

TRADITIONAL ARTS AND CRAFTS

The most characteristic craft forms are embroidery, pottery, and carving. Elaborate embroidery, featuring flowers, leaves, birds, and spiral designs, was traditionally required for the peasant bride's dowry, which might include a dozen ornate pillows and embroidered sheets, two to four decorated feather quilts, and six to eight elaborate tablecloths. Sárköz in Transdanubia, the Matyó region in the Great Plain, and Kalocsa on the southern Danube are especially well-known for their needlework. The Szekler people in eastern Transylvania use hides and sheepskins to make thick coats and jackets, which are then elaborately decorated.

Intricate carving is the domain of the men of the *puszta*, who produce canes, whip handles, pen knives, flutes, and pipes of wood and bone, featuring everyday scenes and patriotic symbols. The old plains style of ceramics produces pottery smoked black in the kiln, unglazed and varnished with pebbles. Standard, mass-produced clothes and furnishings have now replaced traditional styles in Hungarian peasant homes, but festivals and special occasions still bring out characteristic costumes.

Embroidery by Hungarian peasant women is some of the finest in Eastern Europe. Embroidered tablecloths and clothing can now be bought from Transylvanian peasants in Budapest and from stalls at holiday craft fairs.

There has been an enormous influx of foreign movies since the opening up of the economy.

CRISIS IN THE ARTS

The advent of a free market system after 1990 was a shock to creative artists. Not only did they now have to worry about the commercial side of their art, but a massive influx of cultural products from the West—everything from the musical *Cats* to romance novels by Danielle Steel and the latest Arnold Schwarzenegger flick—has flooded the market and made it even more difficult for Hungarian artistic productions to compete. This crisis has hit the film industry particularly hard. Although a few films are still being made with foreign investment and some government subsidies, many film technicians and other personnel have been thrown out of work.

The positive side of the change is, of course, the possibility for the Hungarian arts to finally express themselves in complete freedom, without self-censorship or fear. Furthermore, many feel that now creative artists can return to universal themes and pure artistic achievement, thus making Hungarian culture meaningful for all the world. Others, however, wonder whether high quality can be sustained when the artist has to constantly worry about survival. And some even see signs of old habits—state manipulation of the media and self-censorship, now in fear of nationalist rather than Communist taboos—returning, leaving the Hungarian arts stuck between two worlds, without the freedom of capitalism or the material support of Communism.

THE BUDAPEST SCULPTURE GARDEN

After the fall of Communism, many Hungarians wanted to remove all traces of the hated system from their everyday life. The statues put up by the Communists were an obvious target, and plans were made to put all of the capital's Communist monuments in a "sculpture park." But the task

of cutting down and removing these massive figures of granite and bronze proved to be more difficult, and far more costly, than anyone thought. Many people complained that, in a time of increasing hardship, the money should be used for more pressing social needs.

There were also philosophical and political disputes. Some argued that the symbols of 40 years of oppression should be "wiped off the face of the earth"; others felt that they had become a basic and inseparable part of the city's landscape and should be left to stand, along with monuments from previous eras. Russia protested at the "desecration" of memorials to Red Army soldiers who fell on Hungarian soil during World War II. It was charged that the removal of a statue of the 1919 revolutionary Béla Kun was in effect a tribute to the repressive Horthy regime that drove Kun out. One group of veterans of the 1956 uprising got so carried away that it toppled a statue of the Greek goddess Nike because the five-pointed star she carried resembled the Communist red star.

After three years of debate and preparation, the sculpture park opened in the spring of 1993. It holds 58 prime examples of socialist realist sculpture from all over Budapest on a 20-acre expanse. Huge figures of Marx and Lenin, of the traditional socialist worker-hero, of Soviet soldiers, and of obscure Hungarian Communists now have only each other to intimidate. The effect is strange, and can hardly be described as "artistic," but is most definitely a first.

LEISURE

HUNGARIAN LIFE HAS BEEN CHARACTERIZED more than anything by the lack of leisure time. An emphasis on work and the pressures of survival under Communism left little time and energy for entertainment or fun. When they did have a chance, Hungarians tended to react to their burdensome and over-organized lives by retreating to the privacy of family and home life. Younger Hungarians are now more likely to take the initiative to go to rock concerts and organize trips or sporting activities. But middle-aged or older Hungarians still tend to be worn out or in poor health, seeking their comfort in television and from the bottle.

The working population *(opposite)* does not have much time for leisure, having to run from one job to another just to make ends meet. Senior citizens, however, can afford to spend their time playing cards in the park with their pals *(below)*.

COMMUNISM AND LEISURE

Communist leaders in the early years tried to organize and direct the leisure time of the people. There was the "mass song" movement of singing of folk song-like odes to Communism, as well as organized dance troupes and hiking excursions. A "House of Culture" was set up in every village and every district of the larger towns, and offered a constant flow of programs designed to educate and mold rather than to entertain. Vacations were dedicated to work camps or educational retreats. Those who chose to organize their own leisure activities were seen as suspicious loners.

In the 1960s, people's private lives were given back to them, as long as they did not use them to oppose the system. There were still obligatory marches on official holidays and some extra work, but people could and did take the chance to spend time with family and relatives, to celebrate special occasions at home, to relax with music or television, or to attend cultural events. Vacations were also freed for relaxation; most workers took advantage of the very cheap packages offered by the businesses where they worked or their official trade union, which operated hotels at lakes and other recreation spots all over the country.

With the growing economic crisis in the 1970s and 1980s, it became common for Hungarians, especially men with families, to take on second and even third jobs to be able to buy a weekend house or a car, or just to survive. After putting in a normal work day at an "official"

One of the most popular leisure activities is drinking: Hungarians enjoy a drink whenever they have any free time.

98

job, he spent the evening moonlighting at a second job, or plying his official trade for private customers. Weekends were also typically spent working, and vacations from the first job were a prime opportunity to make even more by working at the extra jobs. Thus many worked practically non-stop, their only respite being a drink, which could be had on or off the job. Women worked just as hard between a full-time job and taking care of all the usual family responsibilities.

Young Hungarians, like young people everywhere, are very resourceful and especially in recent years, have been able to plan their own leisure time and recreation. The loosening of travel restrictions allowed many young people to take trips to Western European countries. The increase in contact with the West brought new styles and activities to Hungary, and young people began to organize alternative festivals, gatherings, concerts, and events. Even the Communist Houses of Culture were opened up for yoga classes, jazz concerts, lectures on the environment, and self-help groups. And young lovers needed no one's permission to go for a romantic stroll in the park or along the river.

THE HOUSE-RAISING PARTY

One feature of rural living is the *kalaka* ("KAH-lah-kah") or house-raising party. Like the traditional American barn-raising, extended family members and even the whole village would come together to help a family build a new house. This old tradition gained a new usefulness in the Communist era, when material shortages and the necessity to use personal connections to get goods made this type of cooperation necessary for any large building project. It even spread to the city: young people wishing to bypass the years-long waiting list for an apartment of their own would enlist all of their friends and colleagues to provide whatever help they could on weekends and vacations—often lasting many months—to build their own place. Although it is now possible to simply pay to have a house built if one has the money, a bit of the *kalaka* tradition still survives.

SPAS AND BATHS

Hungary has more than 500 sources of water with a temperature between 95°F and 195°F. Early Celtic settlers, and later the Romans, chose their settlement sites according to the location of the springs. The ruins of the Roman regional capital, located outside Budapest, are called Aquincum, from the Celtic *akink*, meaning "lots of water." The splendid Roman baths were fed by a system of canals and had floor and wall heating. The Magyars also recognized the waters' therapeutic potential. King Stephen had a hospital built at one spring, and later rulers built further installations. But it was the Turks who fully harnessed the land's thermal powers and left behind the network that exists today.

Hungary uses about 200 million cubic yards a year of an estimated resource of 400 billion cubic yards of thermal waters. Thermal treatments include drinking the water and bathing in natural caves, pools, lakes, and elaborately constructed spas. Spas in special locations are recommended for specific ailments, whether arthritis, open wounds, or lung problems; there are even radioactive mud cures. Tourists have flocked to Hungary from as far back as the 17th century to take the cures, and many Hungarian town names are recognizable as former or current spa locations by the suffix *fürdő* or *füred*, meaning "bath." The thermal lake at Hévíz is the largest in Europe, with a surface area of over 500,000 square feet, but this wonder is now threatened by bauxite mining (for Hungary's important aluminum industry), which siphons off half of the water nature previously pumped in and may soon destroy both the lake's healing heat and ecological balance.

The majestic baths of Budapest are a meeting place as well as a spot to relax and ease the day's aches and pains. They used to be a meeting place for lovers, but strict separation of the sexes since Turkish times put a stop to that. At those baths where mixed crowds are allowed, bathing suits must be worn; otherwise, small "aprons" are handed out to cover the essentials. At some baths, chess players concentrate on boards fixed at the level of the water. One may also want to get a massage, or just relax in the steam, or sit and admire the splendid architecture of the spa buildings themselves, which range from Turkish to classical to art nouveau.

SOCCER AND OTHER SPORTS

Hungarians are avid sports fans, and membership in sports clubs and associations is very high: about 600,000 registered competitors in over 3,000 sports associations. Fans avidly read several sports newspapers in order to keep up-to-date on sports stars' contract negotiations, family life, and coaching changes, in addition to their scores and standings.

Soccer is the favorite sport in Hungary. Fans follow both the national league and international matches. Although the level of league play is not as high as in the larger West European countries, Hungary's national teams did very well in the past. Older fans can still recite from memory the names of the players on the legendary national "Golden Team" of the early 1950s. The successes of the "Golden Team" gave Hungarians hope that, though their political and social aspirations were suppressed at home, at least in sport they could achieve greatness.

Aside from soccer, Hungarians closely follow developments in swimming, water polo, gymnastics, and fencing. Hungarian fencing is at the highest international level, and the country's best fencers are national stars. Other sports include volleyball, team handball, bicycling, sport shooting, and basketball, and in winter, ice hockey, skating, and cross-country skiing.

HUNGARY AND THE OLYMPIC GAMES

Hungary's successes in Olympic competition (mainly in the summer sports) are a source of great national pride. Despite its small size, Hungary was consistently placed in the top 10 countries at the Summer Games, and several times took third place. Hungary has won nearly 400 medals altogether, including 134 gold medals, more than France, England, or Canada. Each time the games come around, the country is gripped by the Olympic fever, and headlines across the press celebrate each Hungarian gold medal.

Hungarian Olympic athletes have been especially proficient in modern pentathlon, fencing, gymnastics, wrestling, and water sports. Hungary's swimmers have surprised the world in the last two Olympics, and Krisztina Egerszegi *(below)* and Tamas Darnyi have become national heroes, respectively winning four and two gold medals at Barcelona in 1992. The Hungarian water polo team has taken the gold medal an almost unbelievable seven times, and the soccer team won it three times. The modern pentathlon, combining horse riding, fencing, shooting, swimming, and running, is said to present a similar challenge to that faced by Magyar warriors in times past.

Hungary was one of the founding nations of the Olympic movement in 1894, and the country has participated in every game since the beginning, with the exception of the 1920 Olympics, when the destruction wrought by World War I and political instability prevented it, and the 1984 Los Angeles Games, when Hungary's political leadership forced its athletes to follow the Soviet-led boycott, disappointing the country greatly. Following the tragic events of 1956, Hungarian athletes stoically appeared at the 1956 Melbourne Games and the country placed fourth in the overall medal standing. A measure of national pride was salvaged in the final round of the water polo competition, when Hungary defeated the Soviet Union five to two in a game fought so hard that the water is said to have turned red from the wounds the players inflicted on each other.

Many Hungarians compete in the Olympics as citizens of other countries. For example, the Romanian gymnast Nadia Comeneci, who astounded the world at the 1984 Games, is actually an ethnic Hungarian, born Ilona Kemenes—yet another point of pride for Hungarians.

"HIGH" AND "LOW" CULTURE

Cultural performances and shows are relatively cheap: movie tickets cost around $1, and even concerts by big-name Western rock stars are usually less than $10.

The theater season lasts from September to May. In the summer there are a number of festivals around the country, offering both Hungarian and international or experimental theater. Excellent classical music and opera performances can be seen all year round, and the Budapest Spring Festival draws many foreign visitors as well. Small, "alternative" movie houses and film clubs still abound in Budapest. They cater to students and young people, showing older, "oppositional" Hungarian and other Eastern European films, as well as art films and independent productions from the West. The average movie-goer is more likely to go to a mainstream movie theater to see recent American hits.

The older and less educated people usually stay home to watch television. Almost all Hungarian apartments have a television set, and viewers can choose from three channels. In addition, many apartment buildings have satellite antennas that receive all-European channels in German or English, and premium movie cable services like HBO have begun to enter the Hungarian market.

Hungarians are avid readers, but it has become difficult for publications to survive. Younger Hungarians enjoy fashion or celebrity magazines. The traditional book publishers have barely managed to stay afloat, and from the looks of bookstands, Hungarians these days seem to be most interested in self-help books, science fiction, and romance novels from the West, all translated and published by newly established publishers.

All that Dance is a moving ballet danced to the music of Franz Liszt and Carl Orff. Here, it is performed at the State Opera in Budapest.

FESTIVALS

HUNGARY'S TRADITIONAL HOLIDAYS AND FESTIVALS were based on the religious and agricultural calendars, including saints' days, and planting and harvest days. The Communist system substituted the traditional holidays with "political" holidays marking landmarks in Communist history. Few believed in these new holidays, but all were forced to recognize and "celebrate" them. With the new post-Communist system, these unpopular holidays have been abolished, and the old traditional ones have been returned to their former importance.

BIRTHDAYS AND NAME DAYS

While birthdays are celebrated in Hungary, they are not nearly as important as "name days." The days on the Hungarian calendar are each assigned to a certain Christian name that is commonly known and used. Some of these assigned days, and the tradition itself, are based on religious saints' days, but those names not connected with major saints are given other days, so that every name has a name day. In fact, the most common Hungarian names, such as László, Zoltán, or Zsuzsanna, each have two or even three days assigned to them—Maria has eight! In that case, one of these days is chosen for the child of that name, and family and friends are told to celebrate on that day and not the others. On name days for the most common names, flower-sellers do a fabulous business, and it seems that every second person on the street or subway has a bouquet in hand.

Name days in Hungary are first of all a family occasion. Fellow students or co-workers give flowers and a greeting, and in the evening the lucky Ágnes or János goes home to assembled family members, more flowers, a special dinner, and toasts. Small gifts may be given by the immediate family, but coming together to celebrate is more important. Birthdays are celebrated in a similar way, but with a smaller gathering, and are usually not marked at all by friends or colleagues.

Opposite: **Easter egg-decorating is a traditional skill practiced in villages. Designs reflect local styles.**

Below: **Traditional dress is a regular feature of wine festivals.**

COMMUNIST AND "OPPOSITION" HOLIDAYS

Communist holidays in Hungary marked days important to the Soviet Union and the founding of the Hungarian Communist state. The major ones were April 4, Liberation Day, the date in 1945 when the Soviet Red Army expelled the Nazis and gained control of the whole country; May 1, International Workers' Day; August 20, Constitution Day, the date of the inauguration of the Hungarian Communist state in 1949; and November 7, commemorating the Russian Bolshevik Revolution of 1917. All of these days were public holidays, filled with official parades, meetings, and festivities that workers and students were pressured to attend.

The Communists also tried to take over days that were traditionally important to Hungarians to make them "revolutionary" without being too "nationalist." Thus, on March 15, the anniversary of the outbreak of the 1848 Revolution, there would be an official ceremony, which in later years even featured national symbols like the national red, white, and green tricolor flag. In schools the date was coupled with the Communist holidays of March 21, commemorating the 1919 Béla Kun Revolution, and April 4,

HOLIDAYS IN HUNGARY

New Year's Day	January 1
March 15 National Holiday (1848 Revolution)	March 15
Easter Monday	April
Labor Day	May 1
Whitsun Monday	May
National Day/St. Stephen's Day	August 20
October 23 National Holiday (1956 Revolution)	October 23
Christmas	December 25 and 26

to become "Revolutionary Youth Days," featuring readings of patriotic and revolutionary poems, visits by political figures, and other programs. The point was to recognize these national days enough to convince the people that the Communist system respected their values, but not so much that Communist holidays would be upstaged or people encouraged to further acts of patriotic nationalism.

Despite these efforts, opponents of the Communist system were still able to make national days, especially March 15, into occasions for opposition demonstrations. Demonstrators would meet at an "unapproved" place, for example at the Petőfi statue in Budapest instead of in front of the National

Communist parades required the participation of thousands of young people and involved massive displays of military might, as much to impress the West as to subdue the local population.

Museum, which was the site of the official ceremonies. They would then march to other squares or statues of patriotic importance, chanting slogans or even handing out leaflets. These occasions were attended by a few hundred people, and often resulted in clashes with police. The demonstrators gradually succeeded in changing the meaning of that date into something threatening to the regime. By the end of the 1980s, days connected with the 1956 Revolution, which had been completely taboo under Kádár—October 23, the day the revolution broke out, and June 16, the execution of 1956 Prime Minister Imre Nagy—also began to be marked by opposition demonstrations. The transformation of the calendar became complete with the fall of the Communist system and the reinstatement of traditional national holidays.

COMMUNIST SATURDAYS AND MAY DAY PARADES

One of the ways in which Communism forced allegiance from its citizens was by making supposedly "voluntary" participation in its holidays and festivals in fact a duty that could hardly be avoided. "Communist Saturdays" were Saturdays on which the workers of a factory or enterprise would "donate" a full day of work on their day off to a cause chosen by Party leaders. The cause might be solidarity with Cuba or some other third world "revolutionary" country or movement, or fighting hunger in Africa, or supporting a Soviet peace initiative. But for the Hungarian worker who trusted neither the political leadership nor revolutionaries in unknown parts of the world, the "Communist Saturday" simply meant one less free day with no extra pay to make up for it. Although such work was not officially required, the workers would risk criticism and losing bonuses or other privileges if they did not show up.

May 1 Workers' Day parades *(above)* were a similar story. Every factory, office, and school had its own marching contingent, holding up a banner proclaiming support for socialism in Hungary or for the Soviet Union. Sign-up lists were posted in the workplace and at school, and those who had not signed up the year before knew they had better sign up this time or face trouble. Good students and Pioneers were especially asked to participate as part of the "extra tasks" they were expected to perform to prepare for future endeavors.

When the day arrived, everyone hated the hours of standing, waiting, and marching. But afterward there was the "street ball," organized in a park or the square where the march ended, featuring food, drink, and dancing. In addition, many enterprises held their own parties, so the whole thing was a kind of fair exchange: the people pretended to support the leadership, and in return they were given a good time.

CHANGE AND CONTINUITY

The new Hungarian political order launched in 1990 brought in new national political holidays in place of the Communist ones. The distorted March 15 semi-holiday was made a full holiday with patriotic emphasis. The once-prohibited October 23 observation was also made a holiday and used to mourn the martyrs and victims of both the 1956 uprising and of the whole Communist era. But the highest place in the new set of holidays was given to August 20— which, curiously, had also been the Communists' most important holiday.

The most important religious event on August 20 is the Holy Right Hand Procession. An ornate reliquary holding the relic of St. Stephen's right hand is carried by Catholic priests through the streets of Budapest, while the crowds offer fervent prayers for the future of the Hungarian nation.

The Communists had very cleverly chosen this day to proclaim the Hungarian People's Republic with its Communist Constitution in 1949. Constitution Day replaced St. Stephen's Day. It had also been connected with the summer harvest and had come to be celebrated as the "day of bread." Whereas in the pre-Communist era the village priest would bless a fresh-baked loaf of bread with holy water, the Communists took the same ceremony and made it their own. Instead of a priest, a Party functionary would ceremoniously cut a loaf that had been tied by a ribbon in the national colors. Now August 20 has regained its full national and religious significance and has been reconnected with Saint Stephen. It is celebrated with military ceremonies, political speeches, meetings sponsored by the various new political parties, religious processions and masses, and, as it has always been, by a grand fireworks show.

VILLAGE HOLIDAYS AND FESTIVALS

Traditional holidays in the Hungarian countryside mix religious ceremonies with old agricultural traditions. August and September are the months for harvest festivities, marked by drinking, eating, and dancing in the open air. Major national and local saints' days are also celebrated, and some villages still hold annual fairs where craftspeople show their wares and there are dances and folk music. A saint's day traditionally special for girls and women is Lucia Day (December 13); females are not allowed to work on this day, and Lucia would punish those who dare to try. Lenten or Carnival festivities are not very common in Hungary, but one place where such customs have remained strong is the area around Mohács in the south of the country. The mourning procession or *busójárás* ("BOO-shoh-yah-rahsh") typically features strange costumes, wild and scary animal masks, and the performance of skits to music, ending with a large bonfire and much drink. These festivals probably are connected as much with ancient rituals to drive away winter and with the expulsion of the Turkish occupiers from Hungary as with the beginning of the Christian fasting period.

Unique Hungarian Easter customs go back to pagan fertility celebrations. Boys and young men call on young women in the village and sprinkle

CHRISTMAS IN HUNGARY

The Christmas season starts in Hungary on December 6, St. Nicholas' Day. Children put boots in the window, like the stockings hung by the fireplace on Christmas Eve elsewhere. If the child has been good, *Télapó* ("TAIL-ah-poh"), the Hungarian Santa Claus, leaves the boot filled with goodies—traditionally chocolate, tangerines, apples, walnuts, dates, and figs. If the child has been bad, the boot will contain just a switch with a devil-figure attached, indicating that a beating is in order. Since no child is all good or all bad, most get both the switch and the treats.

The rest of December is filled with school programs, in which parents are invited to come and hear songs, poems, and plays about winter and Christmas. The climax comes on December 24, or Holy Night. This is a night for the immediate family members to sit around a small Christmas tree, eat and drink together, and exchange gifts. On the following two days (December 26 is also a holiday), the family gets together with other relatives to feast and to eat special cakes, most commonly the *bejgli* ("BAY-glee"), a rolled pastry covered with poppy-seeds or walnuts.

A village tradition of the Christmas season is *regolés* ("REH-goh-lesh"), from the name of the ancient songs that children and young men used to sing from door to door, wishing their neighbors good luck and a fruitful harvest in the new year. December 26 and 27 are name days for István (Stephen) and János (John), two of the most common Hungarian names, and so these name days are also incorporated into the Christmas cycle.

The holiday season is topped off by New Year's Eve, which Hungarians call *Szilveszter* ("SIL-veh-ster"). It is celebrated by drinking, music, dancing, and, at the stroke of midnight, eating *virsli* ("VEER-shlee") or wieners. Pork is the traditional New Year's Day dish, as it brings good luck; chicken, by contrast, is to be avoided, as it can bring the opposite.

them with water. In return, the women offer eggs or a token sum of money. This ritual has been transferred to the city, where the water is replaced by perfume sprayed lightly on female classmates. The traditional Easter feast includes baked ham and boiled eggs. Egg-decorating in the village is elaborate and reflects the local craftwork style. Eggs may be dyed and decorated in folk art motifs, glazed, or have tiny horseshoes hung on them.

FOOD

HUNGARIAN FOOD is hearty and rich, meaty and full of cholesterol. Paprika and goulash have become symbols of Hungarian cuisine worldwide, but Hungary's eating habits reflect historical contact with Turkish, Jewish, Austro-German, and most recently, American culture.

THE PEPPER

The characteristic ingredient in Hungarian cooking is paprika, which finds its way into almost every Hungarian dish. We know paprika as a spice, the ground dried red pepper that gives a characteristic flavor and reddish color to most Hungarian dishes. But Hungarians also use the word for any fresh pepper, from the "white paprika," through yellow and red, to the small dark red peppers that set the mouth on fire. Fresh peppers are either sweet or hot; the taste, along with the shape and color, guide the shopper in making a selection. Several different types, as well as the ubiquitous powdered form, can appear in one dish, such as *lecsó* ("LEH-choh"), a common stewed mixture of peppers, tomatoes, and onions, often including sausage and sometimes scrambled with eggs.

Above: **Hanging peppers in a market.**

Opposite: **A restaurant entices diners inside with life-size statues of the cook and barman.**

Paprika appeared in Hungary around the 16th century. At first, it was used only by the lower classes, who could not afford the "genuine" spices imported from the Far East. But it gradually worked its way up the social ladder and, by the middle of the last century, became an essential part of Hungarian cuisine. Ever since, paprika has been considered a typically and uniquely Hungarian spice, and all efforts to cultivate it outside Hungary have failed. The pepper helped Hungarian scientist Albert Szentgyörgyi win the Nobel Prize in Physiology and Medicine in 1937 when he discovered vitamin C in its richest source, paprika.

Goulash is cooked on an open fire at the International Children's Meeting in the summer of 1993.

SOUPS AND STEWS

Hungary's culinary claim to fame, goulash (*gulyás*, "GOO-yash," in Hungarian), although known abroad as a stew, is actually more common in Hungary as a soup. The dish is cooked with mutton, beef, or pork, and there is even one variation called *hamis* ("HAH-mish," fake) with no meat at all. Goulash supposedly dates back to the time of the original Magyar tribes, who cooked meat together with onions and then dried the product to carry with them on their marauding expeditions. The dish was reconstituted later—the world's first "instant" soup. Later, goulash was traditionally cooked in a special copper or cast-iron kettle called a *bogrács* ("BOH-grahch"), hung from a stick over an open fire. (The dish might still be served in a restaurant in a mini-*bogrács* over a flame.)

However, the dish we know as goulash actually resembles more the various Hungarian stews that go by the name of *pörkölt* ("PUR-kult") and *paprikás* ("PAH-pree-kash"). These consist of any meat (pork, beef, chicken, lamb, veal, or—a Hungarian traditional specialty—wild boar), occasionally with mushrooms or potatoes, stewed in fat with onions and lots of paprika, and served over small dumplings called *galuska* ("GAH-loosh-kah"). A *paprikás* is distinguished by the addition of sour cream, which makes it thicker and richer. Side vegetable dishes served with it include spinach, green peas, or cabbage, either stewed or creamed.

A full Hungarian meal almost always begins with a soup of a lighter variety, such as mushroom, cauliflower, or green pea. These soups are made by briefly frying the main vegetable together with a few pieces of carrot and parsley, adding water and later a roux (soup thickener) made from oil, onion, flour, and paprika, and finally a pasta called *tarhonya* ("TAR-hone-yah"), made of flour and egg dough. Other options for the soup course are meat broth made from either beef or chicken, and a Hungarian specialty, cold fruit soup, made from cherries or plums and milk or sour cream. Other Hungarian soups, including *halászlé* ("HAL-ahss-lee," fish soup), *bableves* ("BAHB-leh-vesh," bean soup), and goulash itself, are substantial enough to be a meal in themselves, and are not usually followed by another main course.

HUNGARIAN GOULASH SOUP

1 small onion, diced	paprika powder
$^2/_3$ lb beef or pork, cubed	salt
$^1/_3$ lb turnip, parsley, carrot, and celery	"tubular" pepper (small, narrow, red, and hot variety)
1 lb potatoes, cubed	cumin seed
2 tablespoons oil or 1 oz. lard	bay leaf

Fry the diced onion in the oil or lard in a covered pan and add the meat and a healthy amount of paprika powder. Add salt and water (as much as you want the soup to be). When the meat begins to soften, add the vegetables, cleaned and cut in half. When the meat is almost done, add the potatoes and bring to a boil over low heat. Season with red "tubular" pepper in winter (or green pepper in spring), cumin seed, and bay leaf to taste.

The frond-like objects hanging from the rope across the front of this house are wine-tasting gourds. They are used to take wine out of the barrel to fill glasses.

DRINKING AND TOASTING TRADITIONS

Hungary's "national drink" is a clear brandy called *pálinka* ("PAH-lin-kah"), which can be made from pears (the best one is the William's pear variety), apricots, cherries, plums, grape skins, or "mixed"—to be sampled at one's own risk! Hungarian hosts offer the drink to guests or visitors at

any time of the day or evening, and it is rude to refuse without a good reason. *Pálinka* is best served cold, and is drunk straight from a shotglass (a shot is a single measure, usually an ounce), in one gulp, if possible. *Házi* ("HAH-zee," or homemade) *pálinka*, made by a farmer rather than in a distillery, is especially prized. It may sometimes be replaced by vodka, which Hungarians believe to be a cure for an upset stomach, and is drunk in the same

The frond-like objects hanging from the rope across the front of this house are wine-tasting gourds. They are used to take wine out of the barrel to fill glasses.

POLITICAL DISHES

Some typical Hungarian foods have made their way into the international political vocabulary, as apt descriptions of unique phenomena in the country's political history. Thus there was the first postwar Communist leader Rákosi's "salami tactics," by which he gradually dismantled all of the competing non-Communist political parties, first by "slicing off" a piece (declaring certain leaders to be "reactionaries" and expelling them from political life), then another, and another, until there was no party left. And the political system that developed during the Kádár era is typically known as "goulash Communism," meaning a form of Communism that provided well for its citizens, ensuring "a goulash in every *bogrács*."

way. The new fashion for all things Western has brought gin, French brandy, and all types of whiskeys into many Hungarian shops and homes, but *pálinka* remains the hard liquor of choice for the "true Hungarian."

Two Hungarian wines have achieved international renown: *egri bikavér* ("AIG-ree BEE-kah-vair"), "bull's blood of Eger," is a dark and strong wine from that northeastern valley. *Tokaj* ("TOH-kay"), the sweet white dessert wine made from grapes around Tokaj, along the banks of the Tizsa river farther to the east, has been called "the king of wines and wine of kings" for its prominence at royal tables over the last centuries. The quality, cost, and sweetness of the best *tokaj* wine, the Aszú variety, is indicated by the number of *puttonyos* ("POO-tohn-yohsh") or butts (a measure of the amount of withered, super-sweet grapes condensed down into an essence that is added to the grape juice before fermentation in special barrels) it contains. Other fine Hungarian wines, both red and white, are grown around Lake Balaton, along the southernmost stretch of the Danube, near the towns of Pécs and Sopron.

Learning the Hungarian toast, *Egészségére* ("EH-gayse-shay-gay-reh"), meaning "to your health," is often the initiation into the mysteries of the Hungarian language for the foreign visitor. Glasses are clinked and then drained. However, in the case of beer, the glasses are not clinked because, as legend has it, the Austrians who executed the freedom-fighting Hungarian generals of the 1848 Revolution toasted their success by clinking beer glasses as the fatal shots rang out.

Hungarian wines bring out the full flavor of such Hungarian specialties as salami and goose liver pâté. The finest wine is the "bull's blood of Eger" (middle bottle).

SHOPPING AND DINING HABITS

Hungarians like to buy their foods fresh, doing most of their shopping at the *piac* ("PEE-ahts"), or market. It might be a vast indoor market hall, an outdoor brick-walled enclosure, or just a designated open space, filled by rows of sellers of vegetables, fruits, eggs, cheese, meat, and fish. The sellers are sometimes the growers of the food themselves, but more often they buy produce directly from the grower. Some stalls offer a wide variety of fruits and vegetables, along with a few packaged products; others are filled with mounds of potatoes, peppers, or melons, which they offer for the best price and sell steadily. Elderly women offering a few carrots, onions, or turnips from their gardens fill the spaces in between stalls. The shopper brings a bag and the seller, after weighing out the requested quantity—usually by putting metal weights on a manual scale—dumps the produce into the shopper's bag, right on top of what is already there.

The *piac*—which is closed on Sunday and Saturday afternoon—is a lively place. Sellers praise their wares, shoppers debate whether they really got the firmest tomatoes or the freshest mushrooms, and there is often a beer stand or two full of thirsty customers, and all manner of non-food items are hawked around the outskirts. Western—mainly Austrian and German—chains are opening more and more supermarkets in Hungarian cities and towns, and with their wider and more appetizing selection than the familiar Hungarian ABC chain, are especially popular with those who have more money and less time to search the *piac* for the best bargains. But since fruit and vegetable stands can be found even near bus stops and at busy streetcorners, and most Hungarian families' refrigerators and kitchen storage spaces are tiny, shopping often and buying fresh are still the norm.

Most Hungarians rarely go out to a restaurant except on very special occasions (weddings or the annual office celebration), and prefer to eat at home and go out for pastry and coffee, or for a drink.

The midday meal is traditionally the main one, and it is generally eaten at work or school, in a cafeteria or company canteen. Supper may be a soup, leftovers, or cold meats, served with cheese, bread, tomatoes, and peppers. Weekend midday meals and suppers on evenings when guests have been invited usually involve the preparation of several dishes. Table setting is informal, and the company may eat in more than one sitting if there are too many guests for the small table. Hungarians are, however, not lax about good manners when eating, and small children (or sloppy adults!) are quickly reprimanded if they eat loudly or carelessly.

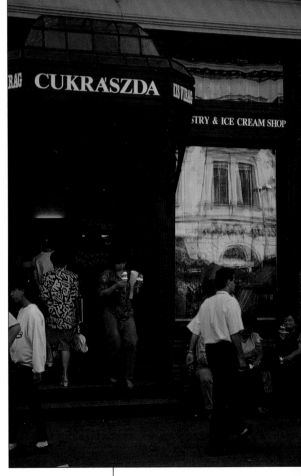

The pastry shop also sells ice cream, which is eaten as a special treat.

Row upon row of pastries and sweets entice the customer in the *cukrászda*.

CAKES, PASTRIES, AND SWEETS

The Hungarian *cukrászda* ("TSOO-krahs-dah"), or pastry shop, is a palace of wonders, filled with creamy delicacies like *rigójancsi* ("REE-goh-yahn-chee"), a chocolate mousse cake topped with chocolate glaze, or *gesztenye püré* ("GEH-stehn-yeh PYU-rai"), a chestnut puree with whipped cream. Poppy-seeds feature in many different Hungarian confections—from pastries and bread pudding to noodles eaten with poppy-seeds and sugar. Coffee was first brought to Hungary by the Turks. Served espresso-style—often in a café called *presszó* ("PRESS-soh")—it is drunk with milk, cream, whipped cream, or sugar.

Another characteristic Hungarian delight, and a favorite of children, is *palacsinta* ("PAH-lah-chin-tah"), a rolled crepe filled with jam, chocolate powder, syrup, cottage cheese, or sweetened nuts, or else an elaborate mixture of several of these. (There is also a savory variety, filled with *pörkölt* or cabbage.) *Palacsinta* is not available in bakeries, but at special stands in resorts, parks, and other places where Hungarians go to relax.

FAST FOOD, HEALTH FOOD, AND THE HUNGARIAN DIET

Political changes and the influx of Western businesses, habits, and tastes have begun to affect the Hungarian diet. Traditional kinds of "fast food," including *lángos* ("LAHNG-gohsh," a plate-size piece of deep-fried dough made from potatoes and topped with salt, garlic, sour cream, and grated cheese), sausage, corn-on-the-cob, and fried fish, have been around for years, later augmented by *hamburgerek* and *hotdogok* (hamburgers and hot dogs). But the arrival of McDonald's, followed by a host of other American chains with their flashy advertisements, English-language signs, and

shiny outlets, has brought a new generation of Hungarians directly into the international "fast food culture." These are not the cheapest places to eat, they may not even be the fastest, and are probably just as unhealthy as many of the traditional Hungarian fried foods, but they do provide young people with a new place to meet their friends that is completely different from places where their parents might socialize.

A trend that has been slower to spread to Hungary is the "health food" craze, with its concern about cholesterol, fat, and meat intake. Hungarian cuisine can be spectacularly unhealthy, featuring pork in high proportions, *töpörtyu* ("TUH-pur-tchew," pork cracklings), *szalonna* ("SAH-lohn-nah," raw smoked bacon eaten straight or with bread), and *zsír* ("ZHEER," pork lard used for everything from frying onions for stews and soups to baking cakes and pastries or spreading directly on bread). These are only mildly balanced by the traditional "salads," which for Hungarians mean pickles, pickled cabbage or peppers, or perhaps sliced tomatoes. Vegetables, if they do appear, are either breaded and fried or cooked almost beyond recognition in a *fozelék* ("FUH-zeh-layk," vegetable stew). In addition, the more exotic portions of animals—like pigs' knuckles, liver, kidney, tongue, cow stomach lining, bone marrow, calf's brain, chicken gizzards, or items called simply "inside parts"—are prized delicacies. The first health food stores, vegetarian restaurants, and muesli cereal could be seen in the capital by the late 1980s, but these fashions have not caught on with Hungarians, and what remains of them are more likely to cater to health-conscious tourists. However, some individually-minded younger Hungarians have become committed vegetarians or, at least, healthier eaters, and there are signs that such new ideas are slowly making their way into Hungary's food consciousness.

A **B** **C** **D**

SLOVAKIA

UKRAINE

Danube

Vienna •

AUSTRIA

Mt. Kékes
(3,330ft) ▲

• Tokaj

• Eger

Sopron •

Lake Fertő

Esztergom •

BUDAPEST •

Debrecen •

Lake
Velence

Veszprém •

Danube

Tisza

Lake
Balaton

SLOVENIA

ROMANIA

Mohács •

• Szeged

Pécs •

Timisoara •

CROATIA

SERBIA

HUNGARY

Danube

Transylvania

● Capital city
● Major town
▲ Mountain peak

Height of land (feet)
over 9000
6000 – 9000
3000 – 6000
1500 – 3000
600 – 1500
0 – 600

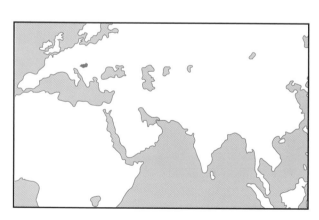

QUICK NOTES

OFFICIAL NAME
The Republic of Hungary (*Magyar Köztársaság*)

LAND AREA
35,907 square miles

POPULATION
10.3 million

CAPITAL
Budapest

ADMINISTRATIVE DIVISIONS
Budapest and 19 counties

NATIONAL SYMBOL
Címer

NATIONAL FLAG
Vertical bands of red, white, and green

MAJOR RIVERS
Danube, Tisza

MAJOR LAKES
Balaton, Ferto, Velence

HIGHEST POINT
Mt. Kékes (3,330 feet)

OFFICIAL LANGUAGE
Hungarian (*Magyarül*)

MAJOR RELIGIONS
Roman Catholicism, Calvinism

CURRENCY
Forint ($1 = 90 forints)

MAIN EXPORTS
Agricultural products, pharmaceuticals, bauxite, machinery, lighting equipment

IMPORTANT ANNIVERSARIES
March 15 (outbreak of 1848 Revolution), August 20 (death of St. Stephen), October 23 (outbreak of 1956 Revolution)

IMPORTANT POLITICAL FIGURES
Stephen I (970 or 975–1038), founder of Hungary; Francis Rákóczy II (1676–1735), leader of struggle against Habsburgs; Lajos Kossuth (1802–1894), leader of 1848 independence struggle; Miklós Horthy (1868–1957), right-wing leader of interwar Hungary; Imre Nagy (1896–1956), executed prime minister during 1956 Revolution; János Kádár (1912–1989), Communist leader from 1956 to 1988; József Antall (1932–), first post-Communist prime minister

IMPORTANT FIGURES IN CULTURE
Bálint Balassi (1554–1594), poet; Franz Liszt (1811–1886), classical composer; Sándor Petofi (1823–1849), lyrical poet and revolutionary hero; Tivadar Csontváry-Kosztka (1853–1919), mystical painter; Béla Bartók (1881–1945), composer; Zoltán Kodály (1882–1967), composer; Attila József (1905–1937), poet; György Konrád (1933–), novelist and essayist; István Szabó (1940–), film director

GLOSSARY

címer	("TSEE-mehr") Hungary's coat-of-arms.
collectivization	The process by which the communist government forced private farmers off their land and into large communal farms.
Communism	Political philosophy asserting that everyone should be equal and should work together for the common good.
cukrászda	("TSOO-krahs-dah") Pastry shop selling ice cream and coffee too.
feudal landholding system	A system in which the peasant is completely dependent on the landlord, must work the land, and is not free to leave the estate.
kaláka	("KAH-lah-kah") Villagers getting together to build a house.
K.u.K.	*Kaiser und König*, German words for Emperor and King. This refers to the period in Hungary's history from late 19th century to the outbreak of World War II.
lakótelep	("LAH-koh-teh-lep") High-rise apartment complex.
Magyars	Ethnic Hungarians.
nationalism	The feeling that people of one's own country or ethnic group are better than others.
nomenklatura	Class of privileged Communist Party officials.
pálinka	("PAH-lin-kah") Brandy made from pear, apricot, or cherry.
piac	("PEE-ahts") Fruit and vegetable market, or flea market.
populism	1930s political movement trying to improve conditions of the peasantry.
proletariat	Industrial working class.
puszta	("POO-stah") Hungarian plain.

BIBLIOGRAPHY

Illyés, Gyula: *People of the Puszta*, translated by G.I. Cushing, Chatto & Windus, London, 1977.

Kopácsi, Sándor: *In the Name of the Working Class*, translated by Daniel and Judy Stoffman, Grove Press, New York, 1987.

Lengyel, Emil: *The Land and People of Hungary*, Lippincott, Philadelphia, 1965.

Life World Library: Eastern Europe, Times Inc., New York, 1965.

Sisa, Stephen: *The Spirit of Hungary: A Panorama of Hungarian History and Culture*, Vista Books, Morrison, N.J., 1990 (second edition).

INDEX

INDEX

INDEX

PICTURE CREDITS
Camera Press: 28, 109
Richard Esbenshade: 1, 16, 20, 38, 39, 40, 41, 43, 45,
   50, 54, 57, 61, 62, 66, 67, 69, 72, 75, 84, 86, 94, 95,
   100, 105, 113, 116, 118, 119, 121
The Hulton Deutsch Collection: 23, 29, 31, 88, 107
Image Bank: 4, 15, 74, 108
Interfoto MTI: 17, 26, 27, 35, 36, 37, 47, 52, 53, 55, 63,
   87, 91, 92, 101, 102, 103, 110, 111, 114
Life File Photo Library: 3, 6, 7, 8, 9, 11, 13, 18, 22, 32,
   33, 44, 48, 56, 58, 59, 68, 71, 76, 78, 81, 93, 96, 98,
   104, 112, 117, 120
Keith Mundy: 5
Liba Taylor: 46, 65, 82, 83, 97